TRIAL

AND

SPEECHES

of

Alexander Berkman

and

Emma Goldman

in the United States District Court in the City of New York July, 1917

Anarchism on Trial

Elibron Classics
www.elibron.com

Elibron Classics series.

ISBN 1-4021-7687-2 (paperback)
ISBN 1-4021-2434-1 (hardcover)

This Elibron Classics Replica Edition is an unabridged facsimile of the edition published in 1917 by Mother Earth Publishing Association, New York.

TRIAL

AND

SPEECHES

OF

Alexander Berkman

and

Emma Goldman

In the United States District Court, in the City of New York, July, 1917

With Portraits

FOR SALE AT THE
MOTHER EARTH PUBLISHING ASSOCIATION
226 Lafayette Street, New York, N. Y.

ANARCHISM ON TRIAL

Speeches of ALEXANDER BERKMAN and EMMA GOLDMAN before the United States District Court in the City of New York, July, 1917

A TRIBUTE

Emma Goldman and Alexander Berkman
        Are in prison,
Although the night is tremblingly beautiful
And the sound of water climbs down the rocks
And the breath of the night air moves through multitudes and multitudes of leaves
That love to waste themselves for the sake of the summer.

Emma Goldman and Alexander Berkman
Are in prison tonight,
But they have made themselves elemental forces,
Like the water that climbs down the rocks:
Like the wind in the leaves:
Like the gentle night that holds us:
They are working on our destinies:
They are forging the love of the nations:

. . . .
Tonight they lie in prison.

JOSEPHINE BELL

(From *The Masses*, Aug., 1917)

Tell all friends that we will not waver, that we will not compromise, and that if the worst comes, we shall go to prison in the proud consciousness that we have remained faithful to the spirit of internationalism and to the solidarity of all the people of the world.

EMMA GOLDMAN

Justice walks with leaden feet and has lost her way and cannot find many of the court-rooms of America.

Ideals cannot be killed by imprisoning idealists. You cannot stop ideas as long as one brain continues to function. Governments, Churches, Judges, and Jailors have tried it as far back as the memory or records of men go. But never have they been able fully to subdue the spirit of man. Ideas are contagious, and crushed to earth, spread over it.

Liberty is never a gift. It is always a purchase, and the price is blood and tears, happiness and the personal liberty of the individual purchaser. Liberty has always been the great temptation for idealists.

We are all walking in the shadow of war. Most of us, however, have our eyes on the stars of peace and liberty, and because a few are articulate, expressing our hopes and desires, Judges are sending them to the penitentiary, to the workhouse, fining them, taking their property, and even ordering them deported to Russia, the new home of democracy. If Christ gave out "The Sermon on the Mount," he would go to the workhouse for six months.

Are some of our courts the new Bastiles, with petty Judges as the wardens? Judges with the dust of dead laws and dead theories in their eyes and mouths and brains are stamping out free speech, are trying to shackle the brave spirits of those who see that the faults of liberty can only be cured by more liberty.

HARRY WEINBERGER

IMPRESSIONS OF THE TRIAL

Oppression has dragged revolt before the tribunal of the Grand Inquisition. Dead words of the Law lay ready as instruments of torture. The District Attorney acted as accuser for the offended divinity. In the box sat the jurors, men with set faces, steadfast worshippers of the dogma. Soldiers and detectives formed nine-tenths of the audience; only a few friends of the accused had been fortunate enough to gain admission to the court.

On his elevation beneath the purple canopy—stretched by another generation—in his solemn high-backed chair behind the huge table laden with law books sat the Judge, the almighty of the hour.

It was the afternoon of the seventh of July, in the Federal court-room situated on the fourth floor of the old Post-office Building in New York.

City Hall Square below was crowded with thousands of people who had assembled to witness the spectacle of the City fathers welcoming the Russian Commission on the steps of the City Hall, just across the square. The Russian tricolor in close embrace with the Stars and Stripes flew from buildings and flagpoles. It was a sunshiny, jubilant afternoon, the Friday which the people of New York had chosen to show their love for the new Russian democracy and to try Emma Goldman and Alexander Berkman for conspiracy.

From the windows of the court-room we could see the festive procession, the waving of flags, the enthusiastic faces that hailed the dawn of a new era, we could hear the music of the band playing that grandest of all songs of liberty, "The Marseillaise," and the cheering of the crowds, who, in the bottom of their hearts, believe in freedom. But the people of New York could not look into the court-room on the fourth floor of the Post-office Building and could not hear the cry of strangled Liberty, nor the strains of the dreadful litany that tells of prison and punishment and death.

The air was heavy, the audience quiet and subdued, the soldiers in their uniforms among the spectators watchful and defiant. The court attendants in their blue uniforms and shining badges used both gestures and looks to intimidate the awed spectators. Officers were posted at the doors to refuse admission to the people of New York who tried to get in.

I sat there at the press table amidst the representatives of our daily papers. Some were older men who followed the proceedings with the mellow superiority of experience. Young reporters were busy making notes, which would never be published.

And there, opposite me, sat Alexander Berkman. A strong, fighting face; decision and action written all over him. Around his mouth plays the tired smile of the fighter who knows what it means to meet stupidity face to face. His hands are clenched, he is armed against attacks and lies, against rudeness and against injustice. He has come to fight. He does not know how to compromise. He does not know how to bow politely to the court, how to invoke in flowery language the attention of the District Attorney or how to arouse the sympathetic interest of his peers—the jurymen. The principles for which he is fighting, which brought about his indictment, are now his only weapons and his only shield. He is a non-conformist who believes in liberty and in freedom uncurtailed in any way.

My memory goes back a few years. I see the very same man surrounded by little children, laughing and merry-making with them. I see him amidst the pupils of the Ferrer School, telling them fairy-tales and admonishing them always to remain brothers and sisters after they have left school and grown up to be adults.

There is Emma Goldman, sitting behind him. I don't see hatred in her eyes but determination; to do to the last minute what she thinks so important for the happiness of future generations. She is reading some report introduced as evidence by the District Attorney. There is a grave seriousness on her features and that wonderful, final resolve that has ever—since time began—caused men to be crucified, to be burned alive, hung, drawn and quartered; the resolve and purpose which have brought to humanity all the good things it possesses.

There is the jury! Twelve men representing the people of New York; the peers of the defendants! I look at their faces: some are old men, some are middle-aged, some are bald-headed and some have gray, black or blonde hair. Some have mustaches and others have not. Some have pepper-and-salt colored suits, others wear suits of brown, black or light-gray. Sometimes they look at the defendants. When they do, it is not for long. It is the casual look at something repulsive, at something that one might be curious enough to look at though one knows that it is bad because it is so different from what newspapers print and politicians praise.

These representatives of the people of New York let their eyes rest with an expression of content upon the District Attorney, that Archangel who guards the gates of their Paradise. Some of the jurors dare, now and then, to glance shyly up at the judge's throne beneath the purple canopy.

His Honor seems uncomfortable in the clear rays of the sun which pour in through the shining window panes onto his face. He must face the sun because his duty compels him also to face the jury and the defendants. He is seated and only his head can be seen above the table, his head on his broad shoulders. A thick, sensitive upper lip, between nose and forehead an angle of about 160 degrees, a small chin, big jaws, his eyes hard, not by experience but by purpose. He seems to me to be a man who would really go and do what you bade him do or what he thought was expected of him.

Now he rises. The black toga of his office seems too heavy upon his shoulders and he throws it back with a tired gesture. Or does he feel too warm? His arms are very short and he is a little man.

I try to read his face. I am very near him. I search for something in his eyes. Nothing is written upon his face, nothing in his eyes.

The witnesses! Everybody in the court-room knows that the District Attorney must prove what the witnesses have to answer, what the jurymen must decide in their minds, what the Judge will pronounce as sentence. . . a dreadful monotony —an iron ring presses tighter and tighter around our heads.

The District Attorney is reading part of a speech delivered by Emma Goldman to the effect that the people themselves should be called upon to decide whether there should be war or not: the same thing one reads in the *New York American* editorials. A witness is swearing that he has heard her utter such sentences. And, like mockery, from across the Square come the sounds of "The Marseillaise," played in honor of the Russian rebels, guests of the people of New York.

And now! "The Star Spangled Banner." Life comes into the Judge. He rises. He gesticulates wildly with his short arms: "Everybody must rise in the room," he shouts, with a voice which seems unused to give command. The soldiers poke their neighbors, court attendants run about the room pushing men and women into patriotic attention. Some persons refuse to get up. The Judge excitedly issues orders. The objectors are dragged out. Everyone who wears a badge seems eager now to earn his livelihood by bullying people into patriotic attention. . . . All is over. The jurors again sit down indolently in their seats, the witness continues his narration.

Hopeless monotony again! The English anthem is being played outside on the Square, but the Judge does not command us to stand up. We are allowed to remain seated.

* * *

The hall is filled with men and women, well-dressed and well-to-do people, as well as laborers and factory girls. They were not admitted to the court-room and have waited patiently for a chance to see the two people who were sacrificing their liberty and their comfort to secure the joys of life for others.

Below in the Square a procession had formed to take the Russian Commission with flying red banners of the Russian Revolution through the streets of our city and to show the people of New York that democracy is triumphant . . . in Russia.

Monday. Again I sit in my chair and listen to Alexander Berkman, who tries in simple but eloquent words to tell the jurymen what it means to be an anarchist. . . . He paints with vivid colors the beauties of a free democracy without oppressors, without poverty, with beauty and content for everybody. He shows conclusively that the District Attorney had failed to prove him "to be the head of a country-wide conspiracy to resist conscription." He shows that speeches by Miss Goldman and by himself had been delivered on several occasions and that the District Attorney used in his evidence only the one speech where there had been no stenographer present to take it down for Miss Goldman. He points out that the stenographic report offered as evidence is the work of a policeman who has never reported a speech before and who has failed in a test in this very court.

* * *

He finished and the jurymen look with set faces at the District Attorney, with the faces of men who care only for the dogma.

Emma Goldman speaks in her defense.

Her speech goes to the heart of everyone in the courtroom, even of those whose hearts are made sound-proof and who would never permit other gods to take the place of their own gods.

She speaks of the twenty-seven years of her rebellion against existing conditions.

She states her unshakeable principles of independence and of liberty.

Her speech is one of the important documents of our century. It will live as the great plea of our time for liberation from ancient customs and institutions.

* * *

The jury goes out and the jury comes in. "Guilty."

The Judge gives the heaviest punishment he can; these are the worst offenders possible.

The government takes possession of the prisoners at once.

The Judge refuses to grant them time to attend to their personal affairs, to take counsel with each other, and a few hours after the sentence had been pronounced, they are on their way to their prisons.

Emma Goldman to sew women's garments in the prison of Jefferson City, Mo., and Alexander Berkman to do some sort of menial work in the Federal prison at Atlanta, Ga.

Freedom is a great vision. It appears upon the horizon of each of us. Some fear even to look in its direction. It dazzles their eyes.

Some retain the shallow name and use it as a bait to fill their coffers or satisfy political ambition; others cherish it in their hearts.

They are hung or sent to prison.

GUIDO BRUNO in *Pearson's Magazine*

The Trial and Conviction of Emma Goldman and Alexander Berkman

WHEN Emma Goldman and Alexander Berkman, charged with conspiracy to defeat military registration under the conscription law, were sentenced by Judge Julius M. Mayer, on July 9, 1917, to serve two years in prison, to pay fines of $10,000 each, and to be probably deported to Russia at the expiration of their prison terms, United States Marshal McCarthy said: "This marks the beginning of the end of Anarchism in New York." But Mr. McCarthy is mistaken. The end of Anarchism will only be in sight when Liberty itself is dead or dying, and Liberty, as Walt Whitman wrote in one of his greatest poems, is not the first to go, nor the second or third to go, —"it waits for all the rest to go, it is the last."

When there are no more memories of heroes and martyrs,
And when all life and all the souls of men and women are discharged from any part of the earth,
Then only shall liberty or the idea of liberty be discharged from that part of the earth,
And the infidel come into full possession.

The Arrest

Emma Goldman and Alexander Berkman were arrested on June 15, at 20 East 125th Street, New York. At the time of the arrival of the Marshal and of his minions, late in the afternoon, Miss Goldman was in the room which served as the office of the No-Conscription League and of MOTHER EARTH. Berkman was upstairs in the office of THE BLAST. A number of helpers were in the building at the time, including M. Eleanor Fitzgerald, Carl Newlander, Walter Merchant and W. P. Bales. Mr. Bales, a young man, was arrested without a warrant. The raiding party included, besides Marshal McCarthy, Assistant United States District Attorney E. M. Stanton, Lieutenant Barnitz, of the so-called "Bomb Squad," Deputy Marshals Doran, Hearne and Meade, and Detectives Murphy and Kiely, of the Police Department.

"I have a warrant for your arrest," Marshal McCarthy said to Emma Goldman.

"I am not surprised, yet I would like to know what the warrant is based on," Emma Goldman replied.

Marshal McCarthy answered by producing a copy of

MOTHER EARTH containing an article on the No-Conscription League signed "Emma Goldman."

"Did you write that?" asked the Marshal.

Miss Goldman replied that she had written the article, and in answer to another question said she stood for everything in MOTHER EARTH, because, she added, she was the sole owner of the publication.

A few minutes later, the officers mounted the stairs and arrested Alexander Berkman.

In the meantime, policemen were busy searching both offices. They found books and pamphlets written by Kropotkin, Malatesta, Voltairine de Cleyre, Max Stirner, Frank Harris, C. E. S. Wood, Charles T. Sprading, Gorky, Andreyev, Strindberg, William Morris, George Bernard Shaw, and many other writers. They seized everything they could lay their hands on, including a card index, bank and check books, and thousands of copies of MOTHER EARTH and THE BLAST, held up by the Post Office. THE BLAST, which was solemnly pronounced by the newspapers "one of the vilest things ever sent through the United States mails," contained, in addition to Berkman's writings, quotations from Victor Hugo and Edward Carpenter, and articles written by Leonard Abbott and Robert Minor.

After the police had rifled the contents of both offices, the three prisoners were taken down to the street and rushed in automobiles to the Federal Building. They were joined by their attorney, Harry Weinberger. There was no opportunity for arraignment that evening, and the prisoners were locked up in The Tombs.

THE ARRAIGNMENT

On the morning of June 16, Emma Goldman and Alexander Berkman were brought before United States Commissioner Hitchcock. Assistant United States District Attorney Harold A. Content appeared as prosecutor. "These two Anarchists," he said, "are the leading spirits in this country in a countrywide conspiracy to spread anti-registration propaganda." Mr. Weinberger, attorney for the defendants, made a motion for dismissal on the ground that advising anybody not to register is not a violation of law. "Failing to register, no doubt, is a crime," said Weinberger, "but telling people not to do so is certainly not a violation of the law." The Commissioner is old and gray; he looked like a relic of the Dark Ages. He held the prisoners in $25,000 bail each. Weinberger protested against the bail as excessive, but was not able to change the decision. Later, when Weinberger and Leonard Abbott approached Marshal McCarthy and when Abbott protested against the holding of the young man Bales without warrant or charge, the Marshal became violently abusive and ordered the ejection of Abbott from the Federal Building.

The Grand Jury Indicts

The prisoners were held in the Tombs practically incommunicado; it was only with the greatest difficulty that they were able to communicate with any of their friends. Gross unfairness was shown in the matter of the bail. When more than enough property was offered to cover the necessary sum, it was refused by Attorney Content on the ground of petty technicalities. Many friends offered money. By June 21, Emma Goldman was free. Four days later, Berkman was released. In the meantime, the Federal Grand Jury had framed a formal indictment.

Opening of the Trial

The trial began before Judge Mayer on June 27. Judge Mayer is a German, and he has the Prussian type of face. It occurred to more than one spectator that the defendants, charged with the "crime" of fighting Prussianism in America, were being tried before a Prussian judge. They announced, at the outset, that they had decided to conduct their own cases. They made it clear that this decision was not in any way to be construed as a reflection upon their lawyer. Mr. Weinberger, indeed, had consecrated himself to this case with conspicuous idealism, and was still giving advice and suggestions. But they had decided that, as Anarchists, it would be more consistent to go into court without a lawyer.

The defendants asked for a postponement on the ground that they had so recently been released from prison that they had had no opportunity to summon witnesses and to familiarize themselves with their case. They also asked for a postponement on the ground of Berkman's physical condition. He had sprained his leg, prior to his arrest, and appeared in court on crutches. Both of these requests were denied by the Judge. He insisted upon an immediate trial. Emma Goldman and Berkman were at first so incensed by the injustice of this decision that they declined to take part in the proceedings. The trial, as Emma Goldman put it, was a farce. Later, however, the defendants consented to examine the talesmen.

For three days the examination proceeded. It is certain that never before in a court of "justice" had there been such a questioning of talesmen, and it is to be hoped that some of those who listened, or answered, learned something about *real* justice and social ideals. Alexander Berkman, who took the lead in the questioning, created an atmosphere that was libertarian and anti-militarist. Among the questions asked were:

"Do you believe in free speech?"

"Do you believe in the right to criticize laws?"

"Do you believe that the majority in a community is necessarily right?"

"Would you be biased against the defendants because they had been active in the labor movement?"

"Would you be biased because they had fought conscription?"

"Do you feel that you would be unable to render a just verdict because the defendants are anti-militarists, or Anarchists?"

"Do you know what Socialism and Anarchism mean?"

"Have you read any Socialist or Anarchist books?"

"Have you attended any Socialist or Anarchist meetings?"

Incidentally, Emma Goldman and Berkman managed to convey a great deal of information bearing on the libertarian struggle in many countries. Robert Emmet was mentioned, and George Washington. The birth control movement came in for discussion.

The court-room was packed with friends of the prosecution, but many friends of the defendants were excluded. Some were roughly handled. June 27, it happened, was Emma Goldman's birthday, and, during the lunch hour, some comrades presented her with a bouquet of red roses.

On June 29, just as the jury was selected, a number of telegrams were received by the defendants from their friends, among them the following from Charles Erskine Scott Wood, of Portland, Oregon. Mr. Wood is a Single-Taxer, poet and art connoisseur, and was at one time colonel in the United States army.

"I have wired the judge and attorney general and prosecuting attorney, and please say to Emma I can be quoted as believing with her that conscription utterly belies democracy, and punishment for criticising the government marks an autocracy in spirit, no matter what the form. Thousands here share this view."

The Case of the Prosecution

On Monday morning, July 2, Prosecutor Content opened his case. He said he would show that the two defendants, whom he characterized as "disturbers of law and order," had both tried in their writings and in their public addresses to influence the ignorant amongst the men of military age not to register. The first witness that he put on the stand was Miss Fitzgerald. He questioned her regarding the No-Conscription League and the "profits" of THE BLAST. She answered him that she and her colleagues had worked for the sake of principle and not for profits. Mr. Content went to the trouble of presenting newspaper reporters, printers, binders, etc., to testify as to the contents, printing and binding of MOTHER

EARTH, THE BLAST and No-Conscription literature; but all this, as the defendants pointed out, was superfluous. They admitted the authorship of the writings which were the basis of the Government's case. Berkman looked the student, the intellectual, with his black-rimmed eye-glasses. Emma Goldman was constantly on her feet, parrying unfair questions, elucidating doubtful points.

One of the witnesses that Mr. Content put on the stand was a police stenographer who testified that in her speech at Harlem River Casino on May 18, Emma Goldman used the words, "We believe in violence, and we will use violence." But Emma Goldman denied ever having used any such words, and she was able to call many witnesses who corroborated her statement. This led to lengthy discussion of the entire question of violence and of violent methods as a means of advancing Anarchist propaganda. Emma Goldman and Berkman read to the jury extracts from articles on this subject, appearing in MOTHER EARTH. The stenographer who reported the Harlem River Casino meeting was shown to be untrustworthy. Another stenographer testified, incidentally, that Emma Goldman was the best speaker he had ever heard. The proprietor of the Harlem River Casino, called by the prosecution, gave testimony favorable to the defendants. He said that the meeting of May 18 had been perfectly orderly, in spite of the fact that a group of soldiers, carrying a flag, had tried to make trouble. A Sergeant of the Coast Guard, appearing on the witness-stand in uniform, confirmed this testimony.

During the examination of several of these witnesses, a military band was playing beneath the open windows, and patriotic speeches, punctuated by applause, could be heard. In the street below, a recruiting station had been established. By a curious irony of fate, militarism and anti-militarism, each in its most dramatic phase, had been set in juxtaposition.

BERKMAN OUTLINES THE CASE OF THE DEFENDANTS

Alexander Berkman, when he came to present to the jury the line of argument on which he proposed to build his case, said in substance: "We admit that we are opposed to militarism and to conscription. We have been carrying on an anti-militarist propaganda for twenty-five or thirty years. But we did not conspire, and we did not advise people not to register. The No-Conscription League refused to commit itself to a policy of definitely advising young men not to register. We decided to leave the matter to the conscience of each individual." All this was substantiated by the testimony of a conscientious objector who declared that he had gone to the office of the League for definite counsel and had been unable to get such counsel. It was further confirmed by a letter of Emma Goldman, referred to by Miss Fitzgerald. In this letter Miss Goldman said that so long as she was not in danger of arrest under the registration law, she would not advise young men not to register; she added that, as a matter of principle, she would not tell a man to do a thing or not to do a thing, "because if I would have to tell him what to do, he would have no strength of character and courage to stand by what he is doing." The position of Emma Goldman and of others connected with the League was: "Each man must decide the issue for himself. As a conscientious objector, he has to decide for himself." Anna Sloan, Helen Boardman, Rebecca Shelly and Minna Lederman all testified that they had never heard Miss Goldman urge violence or non-registration.

The Mysterious $3,000

When the offices of the No-Conscription League were raided by the police, a newspaper published an account of a mysterious bank deposit of $3,000. It was hinted that the money had come from pro-German sources. On July 5, James Hallbeck, eighty years old and a native of Sweden, testified that he had given Emma Goldman a check for $3,000 as a contribution to her work. So the "pro-German" bubble was pricked.

Reed, Steffens, Hall

John Reed and Lincoln Steffens, magazine writers, testified that they had known Emma Goldman and Berkman for many years, and that they did not regard either as "violent." Bolton Hall, Single-Taxer and writer, said that he was a member of the Free Speech League. Asked by the Judge what the principles of the League are, he said:

"It believes in activities tending to promote liberty, and particularly free speech. We have long fought for free speech. We do not believe in putting any restraint on it. We hold that limiting free expression of opinion is the best way to foster insurrection. We are never afraid to listen to any expression, even if we believe it wrong, but we have decided that the individual must bear the consequences for anything he utters."

"Does that mean that you permit free speech even when it is opposed to law?" queried Judge Mayer.

"We believe the constitutional guarantee of free speech makes free speech of every kind permissible," said Hall.

"In other words, the League permits free speech though it may be contrary to existing statutes," the Judge again asked.

"I think that is free speech," Hall retorted.

Hall asserted he had always known Emma Goldman believed in educational work, and in benefiting people through educational activities. He said he had never known her to advocate violence, or to deny any principle which she preached.

Leonard D. Abbott Testifies

Leonard Abbott, Chairman of the Ferrer Association and President of the Free Speech League, was sure that Emma

Goldman had not urged violence at the Harlem River Casino meeting. He said that he had expected she would take a more extreme attitude than she did take. Questioned by Berkman in relation to the educational work of the Ferrer Association, in which both Emma Goldman and Berkman had had a share, Abbott spoke at some length of the Children's School in Stelton, New Jersey, created as a memorial to the Spanish martyr, Francisco Ferrer.

"Does the Ferrer School teach children to disobey the laws of the country?" Mr. Abbott was asked.

"It teaches them," he replied, "to criticise all laws and to prepare themselves for a Free Society."

"When you speak of criticising laws, do you include the laws of this Government?" Judge Mayer asked the witness.

"Yes," was the reply.

"Why was Francisco Ferrer executed by the Spanish Government?" the Judge asked the witness.

"He was executed because he loved liberty and human rights," said Abbott.

"Wasn't he executed upon false testimony?" asked Miss Goldman, springing to her feet.

"Yes," was the reply.

Martial Music Gives Color to the Trial

Revolutionary and patriotic music clashed toward the end of the trial. At one moment the clear strains of the Marseillaise floated in through the open windows from bands accompanying the Russian Commission, which was marching past City Hall with its streaming red banners. This happened just as Miss Goldman read from her writings passages to the effect that war was only in the interests of the working class when it aimed at the overthrow of the capitalist system. When she read her "New Declaration of Independence," setting forth the right of the masses to overthrow a tyrannous and iniquitous government, the band suddenly burst forth with the "Marche Militaire," France's new song of revolution and freedom.

Twice the bands played "The Star-Spangled Banner." Everybody was ordered to rise. The first time, a young girl refused to do so, and was ejected by court attendants. The second time Stephen Kerr and another man were led from the room for refusal to stand, whereupon the Judge said: "Any man who refuses to stand will be taken from the room, and will not be permitted to come back." Emma Goldman and Alexander Berkman remained seated.

Closing Scenes of the Trial

The trial occupied eight days and came to an end on Monday, July 9. Alexander Berkman spoke for two hours. Emma Goldman then spoke for something over an hour. Mr. Content summed up for the Government in a speech not quite an hour long.

The Verdict of the Jury

After listening to the speeches, the members of the jury filed out of the court-room. They deliberated for thirty-nine minutes. It was late in the afternoon. Judge Mayer came into the court-room at 6 o'clock. The Clerk called the roll of the jury, and then turned to Frank M. White, the foreman, and asked him if a verdict had been agreed upon. Mr. White replied that the jury had agreed.

"What is your verdict?" the Clerk asked.

"Guilty," the foreman replied, in a voice that could be heard in the corridors.

Emma Goldman was immediately on her feet.

"I move," she said, "that this verdict be set aside as absolutely contrary to the evidence."

"Denied," replied Judge Mayer.

"I then ask that sentence be deferred for a few days, and that bail be continued in the sum already fixed in our case," Miss Goldman added.

"Motion denied," said the Judge.

The clerk then took the pedigrees of the defendants. Berkman said he was born in Petrograd about forty-seven years ago, that he was single, and not a citizen of the United States. Miss Goldman said she was born in Kovno, Russia, in 1869, was single, and that she was not a citizen by application, although, she added, her father had died an American citizen.

The Prisoners Sentenced

Judge Mayer announced that he was about to impose sentence and asked the defendants if they knew of any reason why sentence should be deferred.

"I think it only fair to suspend sentence and give us a chance to clear up our affairs," Berkman said. "We have been convicted simply because we are Anarchists, and the proceeding has been very unjust." Emma Goldman also protested against the way in which they were being railroaded to prison.

Then came the sentence. Judge Mayer stood, while the defendants remained seated.

"In the conduct of this case," said Judge Mayer, "the defendants have shown remarkable ability, an ability which might have been utilized for the great benefit of this country had they seen fit to employ themselves in behalf of this country rather than against it. In this country of ours, we regard as enemies those who advocate the abolition of our Government, and those who counsel disobedience of our laws by those of minds less strong. American liberty was won by the forefathers, it was maintained by the civil war, and to-day there are the thousands who have already gone, or are getting ready to go, to foreign lands to represent their country in the battle for liberty. For such people as these, who would destroy our Government and nullify its laws, we have no place in our country. In the United States law is an imperishable thing, and in a case such as this I can but inflict the maximum sentence which is permitted by our laws."

The Judge imposed a penalty of two years in prison, with a fine of $10,000 in each case. He instructed Mr. Content to communicate the record of the conviction to the immigration authorities for such action as those authorities might see fit to take when the prisoners had served their terms. Under a new Federal law an alien, twice convicted of a crime, may be deported by the Government to the country from whence he came.

As the Judge finished pronouncing sentence, he declared the court adjourned and started to leave the bench. Emma Goldman at once arose.

"One moment, please." Judge Mayer turned and faced her.

"Are we to be spirited away in a speedy manner? If so, we want to know now, right now," she said.

"You have ninety days in which to file an appeal," replied the Judge.

"Well, how about the next hour or so?" Miss Goldman demanded.

"The prisoners are in the custody of the United States Marshal," Judge Mayer answered, and for the second time he started to leave the room.

"One more word," Miss Goldman said, "I want to thank your Honor for refusing us the two days which are given even to the most heinous of criminals."

RUSHED TO PRISON

The prisoners were spirited away, by midnight trains and with indecent haste. Emma Goldman was taken to Jefferson City, Mo.; Alexander Berkman to Atlanta, Ga.

The vindictive sentences inflicted upon them and the injustice of the entire trial can only have the effect of strengthening the libertarian and Anarchist movement in America.

Their imprisonment is likely to accomplish even more for the no-conscription movement and for anti-militarism than their agitation. The very fact that they are behind the bars ought to make clear to even the dullest mind that the Prussianism that America has set out to combat, by force of arms, is already enthroned in this country.

The crime of Emma Goldman and Alexander Berkman was that they fought for liberty.

Their heroism consists in their willingness to make what even the militarists admit is the supreme sacrifice—the sacrifice of their own bodies and of their own freedom.

It is marvelous to think that Alexander Berkman, after serving fourteen years in a Pennsylvania prison with spirit unbroken, is still willing to go to jail again in behalf of the liberties of the people.

The example of Emma Goldman and Alexander Berkman is inspiring, and will serve as a beacon light for many a year to come.

LEONARD D. ABBOTT

OPENING SESSION

PROSECUTOR H. A. CONTENT: Where is your attorney, Mr. Weinberger?

ALEXANDER BERKMAN: We will conduct our own case. I move an adjournment on the following grounds: We have had absolutely no chance to familiarize ourselves with the case, or with the charges brought by the prosecution against us. We have been unable to see or to subpoena witnesses, many of them being out of town. We have been released from jail only a very short time ago, owing to the fact that it was most difficult to secure for the defendant Emma Goldman the excessive $25,000 cash bail demanded by the District Attorney; owing, further, to the fact that the prosecution placed many obstacles in the way of releasing the defendant Alexander Berkman on bail. Emma Goldman has been out only since Thursday evening. Every moment of her time until Monday night was devoted to securing bail for the defendant Alexander Berkman. As a result of this we have had no time for a consultation, nor any opportunity to familiarize ourselves with the indictment. For these reasons we ask for a reasonable adjournment to prepare our defense.

MR. CONTENT: Your Honor will understand that whereas it is always the defendant's right to defend himself or herself, on the other hand up until this moment Mr. Weinberger was the attorney of record. This is a form of indictment Mr. Wienberger ought to know and knows. He was furnished with a copy of the indictment the day it was filed. He has had ample opportunity to look it over, and it is not very different from other indictments in which he has been counsel.

EMMA GOLDMAN: I wish to state it is not true, as claimed by Mr. Content, that Mr. Weinberger has charge of our case. He is not in charge of our case, not because he would not have been willing or glad to appear, but because we decided to conduct our own case. We wish to conduct our own case, and we feel we ought to have a reasonable adjournment to prepare our defense. We are asking for a reasonable adjournment.

ALEXANDER BERKMAN: I should like to add to the reasons given by Miss Goldman that I have been out of jail only since Monday evening. Today is Wednesday morning. It was a physical impossibility for me to do anything to become familiar with the indictment, look up witnesses, or to give the matter much thought. I was held twelve days in jail, suffering great pain because of the accident to my foot, and I am now physically and mentally not in a condition to go ahead with the trial.

THE COURT: When this case first came up, I stated that the case would proceed today. The statute of May 18, 1917, provides that violations thereof shall have precedence on the criminal docket. That is the mandate of Congress, approved by the President of the United States. You have concluded to conduct your own case, which is your absolute right; and every effort will be made to give you the fullest opportunity to conduct your own case in accordance with law. But I deem it my duty to deny the motion, and the case will proceed.

ALEXANDER BERKMAN: May I say something with regard to the Act under which we are indicted? I am not familiar with it, but I take it that that statute does not intend to deprive us of the opportunity to prepare our case.

THE COURT: I have ruled, Mr. Berkman.

EMMA GOLDMAN: May I also say, your Honor, that I presume that it is not the intention of the Court to persecute us—that as long as we are not familiar with the indictment, or with the various phases of the law, have we not the right to ask you to reconsider your denial of the motion, and grant us a reasonable adjournment for the purpose of familiarizing ourselves with the indictment and preparing an adequate defense? That is a thing which was granted prisoners even in Russia under the Czar. Surely we ought to have this right in the United States.

The Court again denies the motion for adjournment, and jury is called.

MR. CONTENT: Do you want to examine the jurors?

EMMA GOLDMAN: I don't wish to participate in this farce.

MR. CONTENT: Then you don't want to examine any jurors?

EMMA GOLDMAN: No, I don't.

MR. CONTENT: Mr. Berkman, do you desire to examine any of the jurors in this proceeding?

ALEXANDER BERKMAN: I should like to find out first how we are going to be tried, since we are not prepared. I have stated that I got out of jail Monday, five o'clock in the evening. *I am out of prison only one day*, and it was humanly impossible to get ready. I have not even read the indictment yet.

THE COURT: I have answered all that. I have ruled that you have had plenty of time.

ALEXANDER BERKMAN: But I have not had.

THE COURT: I have so ruled and you have an exception, and you say you will conduct your case, each of you.

EMMA GOLDMAN: Since we realize that the trial will

be a still greater farce if we allow ourselves to be tried without an examination, we will examine the jurors *under protest.* We want it to go into the record that we protest against any procedure which makes it impossible for the defendants to study their case, or familiarize themselves with certain technicalities which we, as lay people, certainly cannot do in forty-eight hours or even in three or four days. We will examine the jurors under protest.

Examination of the jury was carried on under the greatest difficulty, the District Attorney and the Judge constantly interfering. The Judge and District Attorney took it upon themselves to instruct the jurymen to answer that they "would not be prejudiced against the defendants if their activities were within the law."

Motion for Dismissal

ALEXANDER BERKMAN: The defense wants to make a motion for dismissal on several grounds.

THE COURT: I made that motion for you at the beginning of the case. Before Mr. Content opens you may make the motion if you want to.

ALEXANDER BERKMAN: We move to dismiss the indictment for the following reasons:

(1) It does not charge any crime.

(2) The conscription law is unconstitutional because it involves involuntary servitude in the army, in the navy and in industrial and agricultural service.

(3) The conscription law violates the moral, ethical and religious beliefs of the people of the United States.

(4) The conscription law violates the conscience of the people who are opposed to war on the ground that human life is sacred.

(5) The conscription law is highly immoral and prejudicial to the best interests of the country, because it is not to the best interests of the country to force people to act contrary to their judgment and their conscience.

(6) The United States has not been invaded, nor is it in danger of invasion; it is not in a condition of rebellion, and therefore the law is not of a defensive but of an offensive character.

(7) It is not just to force an American citizen to die on foreign soil against his will, and thus deprive him of the opportunity to die in his own native country.

For all these reasons we ask that the case and the indictment be dismissed.

THE COURT: Motion denied. You may reserve an exception.

ALEXANDER BERKMAN: Exception taken.

Introductory Address by the Prosecutor

GENTLEMEN OF THE JURY: If my recollection serves me correctly, at the time you were examined as talesmen on your qualification as prospective jurors, practically everyone of you, gentlemen of the jury, assented to the statement that you had, at some time or other, served on a jury; so that you doubtless know the purpose of an opening statement in a case of this sort. It is not in any way to furnish evidence. The evidence will come from the mouths of the witnesses and the documents that will be offered for your inspection. But it is only proper in order that you may be assisted in knowing what the witnesses are talking about, that you should know the nature of the charge, and in a brief and concise way what the Government expects to submit to your consideration, that you may later decide the issue of facts submitted to you by the Court.

The general conspiracy section of the United States laws, Sec. 37 of the Criminal Code, in plain English is this: When two or more conspire to commit any offense against the United States and one or more of such persons does any act toward the accomplishment of the conspiracy—what we call an overt or outward act—then the act is complete and that is a conspiracy. Conspiracy simply means two or more persons acting in an unlawful agreement; that is to say, a conspiracy is two or more persons acting in concert in an unlawful plan, either to accomplish something lawful by unlawful means, or to accomplish something unlawful by lawful or unlawful means. If any one of the persons does any act looking toward the accomplishment of the conspiracy, whether he finally succeeds or not, the crime is complete by the commission of the so-called "overt act."

The selective draft law was passed on May 18th, 1917, and on the same day the President duly affixed his signature to a proclamation fixing June 5th, 1917, between the hours of 7 A. M. and 7 P. M., as the date on which people should register as provided by Section 5 of that law. This is section 5 of that law: That all persons between the ages of 21 and 30, both inclusive, are subject to registration except officials and members of the regular army, the navy, the national guard while in the active service of the United States. In other words, all male persons, whether they are citizens or declarants, or aliens, between those ages, are required by that act to register. Some of them may not be subject to draft. For example, a man born in Germany who has taken out his first papers but has not yet completed his citizenship, under the law could not be drafted; but at any rate he must register, because he is a male person between the ages of 21 and 30, both inclusive, and is not a member of the exempt classes.

In addition to that, Section 332 of the U. S. Criminal

Code says that anyone who directly commits an act or who aids, abets, counsels, commands, induces or procures its commission is a principal. So that you will see at a glance that if you go out and kill a man you are a principal, you have committed the act directly. On the other hand, if you committed that pursuant to my persuasion or inducement or assistance I am an aider, or an abettor, what was formerly known at common law as an accessory before the fact. And by this statute he, too, is made a principal. So that the man procuring the killing is just as guilty in the eyes of our law as the man who fired the shot. So that the indictment in this case charges the two defendants Emma Goldman and Alexander Berkman, and a lot of other people whose names are unknown to the grand jurors, entered into an unlawful agreement or conspiracy that a lot of people of conscriptable age, other than those exempted by reason of service in the army, should willfully disobey the sections of the Act requiring them to register, and that the conspiracy further required that these people and the unknown people should aid and abet and assist and counsel and advise, and assist persons to willfully disobey the command to register—though the law provides that it is the duty of everybody to register, all male persons in the United States other than members of the army, etc., to register in the precincts where they shall have their permanent abode. Whether or not the conspiracy was accomplished makes no difference; but the Government will prove to your ample satisfaction that these persons were component parts of an unlawful conspiracy of two or more persons to induce people of conscriptable age liable to register to disobey the law passed by Congress, signed by the President, and in the pursuance of which law the President of the United States duly issued his proclamation; and to accomplish that conspirative act the indictment charges that on the 18th day of May, on the very eve of the day when the President affixed his signature to the bill, this defendant Emma Goldman, at the Harlem River Park Casino, in the City of New York, delivered an address which was an overt or outward act looking to the accomplishment of their unlawful designs.

Further, to accomplish the object of the conspiracy, that the defendant Alexander Berkman on the 1st day of June, in New York City, published or caused to be published a magazine known as THE BLAST, about which some of you were questioned by Mr. Berkman. The magazine itself, the June issue, will be offered in evidence. That on or about the 2nd day of June, a companion magazine known as MOTHER EARTH, or a copy thereof, was handed by Miss Goldman to an *Herald* reporter by the name of Haggerty, who will be called as a witness before you. That further to accomplish the object of the conspiracy on the 4th day of June, on the eve of the registration, these two defendants, in the Hunts' Point Casino, in the Borough of the Bronx, New York City, both delivered addresses, outward acts looking toward the accomplishment of their unlawful designs and plans.

That, gentlemen, is in brief a statement of the Government's case. So that the Government will prove to your satisfaction that at 20 East 125th St., New York City, each of them ran a publication there, Berkman's known as THE BLAST, Miss Goldman's as MOTHER EARTH; that both published a June number which we claim is highly offensive to law and order, and which we claim further was directly published for the purpose of procuring people willfully to set themselves above the provisions of the Draft Act of May 18th. We will show that these two people were at all times in active unison and accord; that they sent out through the mails and otherwise literature tending to the result of resisting by every means in their power the laws of the United States duly enacted by the representatives of the people.

The Government will prove further that these people at public meetings have done their very best to inflame the populace to such an extent that it will defy the laws of the United States in every particular; that all these acts together constitute not only a conspiracy but a violent attempt made by these two disturbers of law and order to induce people wilfully to refuse to register, although the Congress of the United States have decreed that people must register as provided in that act of May 18th, 1917.

There is no occasion for further comment at this time. The facts will speak for themselves. The articles and the speeches made by the defendants will speak for themselves. But bear in mind, gentlemen, at all times, that the charge is this: That these two people were in an unlawful agreement that certain people should wilfully refuse to register, that they should assist in every way and counsel and induce people of conscriptable age in every way wilfully to fail and refuse to register in defiance of the laws of the United States, and to further their unlawful designs they committed many outward acts tending toward the breach of the peace and tending toward the accomplishment of their wicked design.

THE COURT: Before the examination of witnesses is begun, the program will be this: As to any particular witness produced by the Government, one of the defendants only will offer any objections. That objection will be noted on behalf of both defendants. If the Court rules against the defendants, the defendants from now on will be required to take an exception. But an exception taken by one will be for the benefit of both. So that, for instance, witness number one would be objected to by the defendant Berkman or Goldman, whichever they may chose; witness number two the other defendant. But there would not be objections by both defendants at the same time, which would only tend to confusion. The other method that I have suggested, and which I have the discretion to require, will safeguard the rights of both defendants, because both the objection and the exception, if such there be, will be for the benefit of both defendants. Now you may call your first witness.

The prosecution proceeds to present the case of the Government through its witnesses.

ALEXANDER BERKMAN

Alexander Berkman's Introductory Address

After the witnesses for the prosecution had testified, the defense opened its case with the following address by Alexander Berkman.

GENTLEMEN OF THE JURY:

The facts in this case are very simple. It is not a question of printers' bills; it is not a question of rent bills or of deliveries by this or that expressman. The only question at issue here is: Did the defendants conspire to urge people not to register? Before I briefly state what the defense will prove, may I be permitted to make a few remarks with regard to the fact that Miss Goldman and myself are conducting our own case. I merely want to explain our reasons since, so far, our reasons have not been brought out. I want to state right now that Mr. Harry Weinberger is a personal friend of ours, and in justice to him I wish to say that there has been no misunderstanding whatever between Mr. Weinberger and the defendants. We are the best of friends. Mr. Weinberger was our attorney only in the matter of bail; and when the matter of bail was settled, Mr. Weinberger ceased to be our attorney in that connection. Of course, we consult Mr. Weinberger on various questions. But it is a matter of principle on the part of Miss Goldman and myself to defend, or rather to conduct, our own case. As a matter of principle we do not believe in being represented by legal talent at our trial. We believe in explaining things to the jury ourselves. And we believe that it is just and fair to have the jury get some idea about the defendants from their own appearance, from their own expressions of opinion and views. That is all I want to say on this point.

I have stated that the only question involved in this case is whether the defendants conspired to advise people not to register or to urge people not to register. I believe that the Government has absolutely, in fact ridiculously, failed to prove its case. It was brought out here during the examination of the jurymen that the Government must prove its case beyond a reasonable doubt. It seems to me that the Government has not even begun to prove its case that there was a conspiracy between Miss Goldman and myself to urge people not to register. But we, the defendants, take this opportunity to state clearly and frankly to you, gentlemen of the jury, that we are opposed to conscription. I do this so that, during this trial, you may be able to see for yourselves that the defendants are sincere and frank; that they will tell you the truth as to what they do believe and what they do not believe. We will prove that the defendants have throughout their lives always stood up for the things they believe in, no matter whether the majority opinion was against them. And similarly in this case, as in all our past, we mean to acknowledge frankly what we believe, and to be as frank in stating what we do not believe. We will frankly admit what we said at mass meetings and what we wrote in various magazines, but we will just as frankly deny anything we did not say on the platform or in print. We will deny anything put in our mouths by any one, contrary to our wishes or opinions. In short, we will hold ourselves to the facts.

We declare emphatically that we are opposed to conscription, and that we have been opposed to conscription for twenty years or more. We go further: we are and have been opposed to every form of militarism and war. But we deny absolutely that either of the defendants ever told any one not to register. We deny that we were in a conspiracy to advise or to urge people not to register. We will prove to you, gentlemen of the jury, beyond any reasonable doubt that the No-Conscription League, of which these defendants are members, consistently refused to advise people to register or not to register. We will prove to your complete satisfaction that the No-Conscription League took a positive decision, at one of its meetings, to give no advice in this matter, but to leave it to the judgment of each individual to decide for himself.

We will further prove to you that the alleged overt acts charged against us in this indictment were the normal expression of the opinions and activities to which the defendants have been devoted for the last twenty-five or thirty years. We will prove that they were the continuation of an agitation carried on by these defendants against conscription, militarism, and against war, during more than twenty years, and not a matter of any recent happening. We will prove to you that for many years the identical views have been expressed by us against war and in opposition to the forcing of human beings to do anything against their will. We will prove further that the overt acts charged against us were not overt acts at all, but the legitimate expression of independent and fearless opinion.

We will further prove to you that the defendants Emma Goldman and Alexander Berkman have been friends and comrades for many years. That they worked along similar lines of activity, but that they were independent thinkers, and that their activities were always independent: that they used independent methods, and independent platforms, though it often happened that they spoke on the same platform, and published articles in the same magazines. We will also prove to you that the monthly magazine MOTHER EARTH, published and edited by Emma Goldman, always was and is now an entirely separate and independent publication from the labor paper published in San Francisco by Alexander Berkman and known as THE BLAST. We will prove that MOTHER EARTH has existed for twelve years and that it has consistently followed the same policy against war and in favor of universal peace. We will show that THE BLAST was started about a year and a half ago, four thousand miles from MOTHER EARTH, in San Francisco, as a result of special labor conditions on the Coast; that it had absolutely no connection with MOTHER EARTH, and that the circumstance that the last two issues of THE BLAST were published in New York has also no bearing whatever on MOTHER EARTH, but is due to the fact that I had special business in New York in behalf of certain labor unions, and that my stay in New York was unexpectedly protracted and that I therefore decided to publish a few issues of the paper in this city. We will prove that the mere fact that MOTHER EARTH and THE BLAST—and a number of other magazines, for that matter—happened to hold similar ideas on some subjects, does not in any way constitute either an overt act or a conspiracy, but that, as a matter of fact, there is absolutely no reason to assume that there is any conspiracy involved.

We will also prove to you, gentlemen of the jury, and to your entire satisfaction, that the consensus of intelligent opinion in this country, the opinion of leading writers, of public speakers and statesmen, is that registration and conscription are two distinct things, two separate conceptions; indeed, two different issues. In fact, we will prove by intelligent and reliable witnesses that many people believe in registration but are opposed to conscription, on the ground that registration and conscription are different issues.

And finally we will prove to you, gentlemen of the jury, that at no time and at no place did these defendants, or either of them, urge people not to register. In fact, we will submit documents to prove that one of these defendants wrote a special letter to tell the members of the No-Conscription League that she is entirely opposed to advising anyone not to register. We will submit documents to prove that at no time, at no place—neither in our publications, on the platform, nor anywhere else—did these defendants, or either of them, advise or urge people not to register.

DISCRIMINATION AGAINST THE DEFENSE

After Alexander Berkman delivered his introductory address to the jury, the defense called its witnesses.

The prejudice and venom on the part of the Court and the Prosecution against Alexander Berkman and Emma Goldman was demonstrated from the very beginning. It reached its climax in the brutal treatment of the friends of the defendants who came to attend the trial. While the court room was packed with friends of the Judge, Prosecuting Attorney and Marshal McCarthy, the friends of Alexander Berkman and Emma Goldman were shoved about and insulted and on numerous occasions almost kicked down the stairs. It was under only the greatest difficulty that a few friends of the defendants could be passed through the Cossacks at the door of the American Court. On one occasion Emma Goldman had to call upon Judge Mayer for reasons why the friends of the two defendants were thus treated.

EMMA GOLDMAN: Your Honor, is there any special reason why the friends of the defense are kept out, as long as there is room in the court?

THE COURT: The control of the courtroom in such matters is entirely in the hands of the United States marshal. I assume that he is exercising his discretion appropriately.

EMMA GOLDMAN: We certainly protest against the discrimination.

THE COURT: The court has no knowledge of discrimination. How much time do you desire?

ALEXANDER BERKMAN: I think the defense will require about three hours altogether. Maybe less.

THE COURT: Well, endeavor to finish the defense's summing-up by 1:15 if possible.

Address by Alexander Berkman

GENTLEMEN OF THE JURY:

It is for the first time that I rise to address a jury.* It was a new experience for Miss Goldman and myself to examine the talesmen, and it is a new experience to conduct a trial without the presence of counsel. It is more than probable and quite natural that we did not follow the usual procedure. It is also very likely that we have neglected many points and circumstances which a trained lawyer would have used in behalf of the defense. But, as indicated in our introductory statement, it is a matter of principle on our part to dispense with counsel and to address the jury face to face, thus to enable the jury to judge for themselves as to the quality and the character and motives of the defendants. No doubt we could have had the services of brilliant lawyers, and I am sure that even the best legal talent of the country could have been at our disposal. We believe that the fact that we have dispensed with lawyers is to a considerable extent to our detriment. But for the sake

*At his trial in Pittsburgh, Pa., in 1892, in connection with the historic steelworkers' strike at Homestead, Alexander Berkman refused to be represented by counsel or in any way to participate in the judicial farce. He contented himself merely with reading a statement, setting forth his social views and explaining the motive and purpose of his act.

of the opportunity to speak to you, as I have indicated, face to face, we are willing to take that disadvantage, because after all, to stand up for our principles in the expression of our ideas for ourselves is more important, more vital to us than the mere question of liberty or even of life.

Gentlemen, if in the examination of the talesmen we have perhaps asked inappropriate questions, or if in the excitement of the unusual experience we have been guilty of some discourtesy, we wish now to express to you our deepest regret and apology. I am sure that you will not hold our inexperience against us.

And now to the case. The charge against us, as you know from the indictment, is that we conspired to advise and to urge men of conscriptable age not to register. Remember, gentlemen, the indictment is in regard to a conspiracy to urge people not to *register*. If you look through the indictment you will not find a single word about *conscription*. I want you, gentlemen, to bear it in mind that the indictment sets forth a conspiracy and overt acts alleged to be connected, in order to induce young men not to register. The question now is, Did the prosecution prove the alleged conspiracy? Did the prosecution prove that we urged people not to register? Did it prove any overt acts in furtherance of that alleged conspiracy? Did it even attempt to prove or to demonstrate that we are guilty as charged? O no. The prosecution felt its case so weak that it had to drag in a thousand and one issues that have nothing to do with the present charge. It had to drag in the question of Anarchism, of violence, of the Ferrer Modern School, of mass meetings held three years ago under special circumstances, of protest meetings held in this city about four years ago with regard to the Colorado miners' strike, of protest meetings held in connection with the Rockefeller treatment of the Ludlow miners. It had to drag in a thousand and one questions that have as much relation to this case as a lion is related to a jackass.

Why were those irrelevant issues dragged in by the prosecution? Was it not because the prosecution sought to obscure the issue in this case? Was it not because the prosecution hoped to prejudice you, jurymen, perhaps to frighten you, if that were possible, in order to set you up against the defendants, because there is no evidence whatever to prove the charges of this indictment? The prosecution, so far as these defendants are concerned, is perfectly welcome to its professional subterfuges to becloud the issue before you. We don't evade any issue. But the bare fact that the prosecution is compelled to resort to such doubtful tactics ought to be sufficient for any intelligent man to realize that there is absolutely no foundation for this charge, and that we stand here indicted for a charge never mentioned in the indictment itself. *We stand here accused of being Anarchists.* A vain accusation! We *are* Anarchists, and I for one am proud of being an Anarchist, and I am sure I may say the same for my co-defendant Emma Goldman.

You have heard a good deal here about Anarchism and about violence and similar matters unrelated to this indictment. Now, once for all, what is all this talk about violence in relation to Anarchism? I think it is time to explain and to make this matter clear. I am tired of hearing Anarchism confused with violence, the explanation of a thing confused with the cause of the thing. I am tired of all that, and am glad of the opportunity—whatever it may cost—to speak to you, gentlemen, and to tell you just what Anarchism is to Anarchists,—not to the enemies of Anarchism, but what Anarchism is to us and what our position is on violence. There will be no evasion by us. Gentlemen, there is too much humbug in the alleged attitude of the average man toward violence. You speak to the average man, the unthinking man, and ask him, does he believe in violence, and he will hold up his hands in horror. "No!" he will shout. And yet you know it is the most unthinking statement an intelligent man could make. I am sure each and every one of you, gentlemen, is a law-abiding, peaceful citizen. You believe in peace rather than violence. And yet you are all concerned and involved in the present war. You all support the war, which is nothing but wholesale violence. It must, therefore, appeal to your common sense that a sweeping general statement about violence—belief in violence or disbelief in violence—is the statement of an unthinking person. We all believe in violence and we all disbelieve in violence; it all depends upon the circumstances. Under ordinary circumstances no one wants violence, no one wants bloodshed; and yet certain circumstances arise when violence seems to be necessary in order perhaps to combat greater violence, in order to combat a greater evil that may menace humanity. You all therefore, and each of you, do not believe in violence and yet you support the Government of the United States to-day, you support it in the war, a war that means the greatest possible violence. But you have your own good reasons to support this war. I personally do not believe in this war. I do not believe in any war of that character. I believe the war is merely for the purpose of furthering capitalistic interests. I believe the people have nothing to gain from this war, neither the people of Europe nor the people of America. I believe in universal peace. But I am not a pacifist. I am a fighter and all my life I have been fighting for liberty. I am not a pacifist. I want that emphasized. I believe in war under certain circumstances. I believe in fighting. But it is unfair that some remark about violence be picked out here and there, perhaps from the report of a mass meeting held three years ago, an expression used by people who may be dead now, for all I know—yet I am ready to stand responsible, as the then editor of the MOTHER EARTH magazine, for any expression used there. All I want is to explain, explain the meaning of such references.

Now, as to the question of violence. Gentlemen, if you know anything at all about human life, if you reflect on the progress of civilization, you will realize that there are two tendencies in human life, tendencies that have always been the foundation and the lever of all progress. Those two tendencies are: the *constructive* and the *destructive* tendency of man. The greater the intelligence, the higher the rise in the scale of development, the less necessity or justification for the destructive tendency of force and violence, and the greater the need for, and the application of, the constructive efforts of man. Take the primitive man, for instance, the cave man. He rushes out of his cave and grabs the female. He knocks her down with a club and drags her to his cave. He is using—whether he knows it or not—the destructive tendency of man, the spirit of violence, of force, of superiority, of authority. But sooner or later, and indeed very soon, he realizes that he and the female have mutual interests: what is good for one is also good for the other: they need each other. He ceases to use the destructive tendency upon the female—he becomes constructive. They organize the family. And one family fights another family. One family uses its destructive tendencies upon the other, tries to annihilate, destroy it by the use of superior violence and force, until the two families rise a little more in the scale of intelligence and realize that they have common interests which can be furthered better by co-operation than by strife. Then the two families combine, and you have the clan. And clan fights clan for the means of subsistence or domination, until they realize their constructive needs and possibilities, then combine and become the tribe. And tribe fights tribe, until tribe and tribe become constructive instead of destructive, become civilized, and then we have the nation. To-day, gentlemen, the nations have not yet fully risen to the constructive level. They are still destructive. As the primitive cave man fought the female, as one family fought the other, as clan fought clan, so to-day this barbarism still persists and one nation fights another nation with force and violence, with dynamite, with flying machines, with the most ingenuous inventions of the human mind, inventions which should be for the benefit of mankind, not for its destruction. But the time is coming when the nations, like the clans and tribes of the past, will develop their constructive tendencies, will realize that all humanity is kin, and that people in Russia, in Germany, in France or America have the same purpose: to live, to enjoy life and liberty and sunshine. They will learn that it is better to co-operate, to work together, to use mutual effort for a common good, rather than to murder and slaughter each other. The nations that are fighting to-day are still in the *destructive* stage of their development. But we, we Anarchists, have reached the *constructive* stage, and we say to the nations, as we would have said to the primitive men: combine; work together; help each other; mutual aid shall be your condition of life. We are the Internationalists, and I am sure that some day the nations will become international, in the sense that they will do away with all this internecine strife, do away with murder, slaughter, and violence. Yet you accuse *us* of violence—we who stand for the principle of universal peace? Preposterous!

Now, what is the relation of this particular point to Anarchism itself? Of course, gentlemen of the jury, you know that Anarchism is a new idea, comparatively speaking. It often takes hundreds of years to elucidate and explain and make a new idea popular, especially a new idea that runs contrary to all the accepted notions, all old prejudices, all our old superstitions. Anarchism wants to change the false values of hatred, of strife, of brother murdering brother, the false values of exploitation and robbery, of tyranny, of oppression. We want to change these false values and give humanity new values. In the words of the great, perhaps the greatest, philosopher of modern times, we want to trans-value all human values, to give them a new meaning, a new foundation, with the hope and the necessary result of a different and better society. Anarchism has been misrepresented. Naturally so. As many philosophies, that are accepted to-day, had been misrepresented in the past. What is the matter with Christianity itself? You remember the early Christians in the time of the Roman Caesars, the Christians who stood for an ideal then as we stand for an ideal of brotherhood to-day. What did they do with those Christians, Mr. District Attorney? They put them in the arena to be torn by wild beasts. They crucified them on the streets of Rome, because crucifixion then was the customary method of capital punishment. And if we had crucifixion to-day, I am sure that these defendants would be crucified also. What did they do with the Hugenots, the conscientious objectors of their time? You know. They slaughtered the Hugenots by the hundreds of thousands all through France. And what did they do with Garibaldi whom the City of New York has been celebrating only a few days ago? There is his statue. What did they do with Garibaldi, the liberator of Italy from the yoke of the foreign oppressor? They put him in prison. What did they do to Mazzini and the other great liberators of Italy? They put them in prison. What did they do with Bruno who propagated a new and strange and unpopular theory? They burned Bruno at the stake. And I am sure that there are men to-day who would burn the modern Brunos at the stake. And a hundred years hence their descendants would build monuments to them, as you have built a monument there for Garibaldi.

We do not need to go back very far in history. What is the matter with the Russian revolutionists? Their Commission is honored by your city right now, at this very moment. I say that their Commission honors your city. The representatives of the Russian Revolution, the revolution fought against the tyranny of the Czar, the revolution whose great gospel is liberty for all, well-being for each, happiness for humanity, that revolution has to-day its representatives in your midst and you are honoring them. And who are those revolutionists? They have returned from Siberia, from the dungeons of the Peter and Paul Fortress, they have returned from Schluesselburg, from the mines of Kara, from Sakhalin, from the places where revolutionists were sent by the Czar and governors of Russia for a hundred years. These rebels against tyranny, these lovers of humanity have come back from Siberia and to-day they are at the helm of the destinies of Russia. You celebrate them to-day in the persons of their representatives, and *we*, we are here in this courtroom, on trial—for what? For loving humanity.

I said it would be interesting to know on this occasion, especially because it is in the evidence, what relation violence has to Anarchism. You have heard the word Anarchism mentioned many times, but perhaps you have not heard what it really means. It comes from two Greek words, and very simple they are. "Arche" means power or violence. And "an", a prefix, means without. "Anarche" in Greek, Anarchy in English, which means without violence. The philosophy of Anarchism means the negation of violence, opposition to violence. The very translation of the word means absence of violence and absence of government as representing organized forms of violence. And yet this stupid man, the ignorant man opposite me, dares say Anarchism means violence, when the very meaning of the word Anarchism stands for the negation of all forms of violence and force. I have tried to call your attention, gentlemen, to the fact that Anarchism, which stands for human brotherhood, for the constructive tendencies of man, seeks an opportunity only, an opportunity to develop these tendencies of man, these constructive tendencies as against the destructive tendencies; an opportunity to develop them first, of course, by enlightening the people, by telling them what Anarchism really means, by doing away with all those misrepresentations of Anarchism which our enemies have inculcated into the minds of the people. Misrepresentations—and when was there a time when a new idea was not misrepresented? Why, some of you perhaps remember the

Abolitionist days in this country. Did not the ordinary stupid citizen consider an Abolitionist a murderer? Why? Because those who were their enemies, those who were opposed to their ideas misrepresented the abolitionists, misrepresented the philosophy and vilified the champions of that philosophy. And what did the abolitionists want? They wanted the emancipation of the black man. To-day it is a fact. They were successful finally. We have not been successful yet. But before they were successful what happened to the greatest, to the noblest representatives of abolition? What happened to Garrison, William Lloyd Garrison who was dragged in the streets of Boston, dragged by a mob and almost lynched because he stood for a bigger conception of human love, because he stood for a greater conception of brotherhood, because he said "No country can be free when half way free and half way slave."* And we, gentlemen of the jury, say the same thing to-day. No country is free, half way free and half way slave. We are in the position of Garrison and Wendell Phillips and John Brown. But we say that not only the black slave must be emancipated, but also the white wage slave of the factory. We are the *modern* Abolitionists.*

But why do some people pretend that we mean only violence? When we explain what violence is, where violence comes from, and how inevitable it is that when there is violence above there will be a réaction, there will be violence below—when we *explain* these things there comes the District Attorney and says, "They *advocate* these things." If I say to you, "It looks cloudy and there is going to be a storm," will you say that I have caused the storm or that I am responsible for it? That is the logic of the District Attorney.

Gentlemen of the jury, in looking over the testimony in this case it strikes me, and I am sure it will convince any intelligent man, that the District Attorney proved only one thing, and that is that we are Anarchists. It did not need to be proven, Mr. District Attorney. We cheerfully, proudly admit that we are Anarchists, that we are opposed to all capitalist wars, that we believe in universal peace, that we believe in brotherly co-operation, in mutual aid, not only in the family and the tribe and the clan and the nation, but between all nations, between all humanity. We stand here as Anarchists, and I am proud to stand here as a believer in the highest ideal that the human mind ever conceived, the ideal of liberty and sunshine for everyone: the ideal of the rights of the child, the child who to-day works in the factories and the mills, and is exploited day after day; the rights of the woman, the equal rights of the woman in every way; the right of the man not alone to an empty political liberty, but the right of every man to the resources of life, the right of the working class to produce for the general benefit, not for the profit of this or that monopolist; the right of humanity to enjoy the wealth of the world. What is wealth for? Why was it produced? It was produced to enjoy, not to speculate with, not to monopolize. We demand, in other words, the emancipation of the wage slave, white or black, the factory slave, the working class, the proletariat—as we call them—the proletariat of all countries. I have no more use for the exploiter and monopolist of America than I have for the exploiter of Germany or Austria, of Italy, South America or China. The exploiter of humanity does not belong to a particular country. It is an international class. The true benefactor of mankind is also international. It is the man or the woman who works for greater liberty and well-being, the people who advocate peace, brotherhood among humanity. We, the Anarchists, stand for the emancipation of the wage slave from slavery, for the liberation of the woman and child from exploitation. We demand for every man, woman, and child the right of life, the opportunity to work and produce, and a chance to enjoy sunshine and happiness. That is what Anarchism means.

The District Attorney has proven that we are Anarchists, and I want you to know what we Anarchists stand for. What else has the District Attorney proven? He was to prove two things, gentlemen. He was to prove that there was a conspiracy between these defendants, a conspiracy to advise and urge conscriptable men not to register; and he was to prove that overt acts had been committed by us in pursuance of that conspiracy. Has he proven either one of these two propositions? He has not proven a single thing about either one, neither the conspiracy nor the overt act. And when I go ahead to analyze his testimony and our testimony, I think I can convince you, gentlemen, beyond a reasonable doubt that we have proven our case instead of the District Attorney proving his. You have heard here, gentlemen, that on your oaths you cannot convict unless you are absolutely certain in your own hearts and consciences that the District Attorney has proven his case beyond a reasonable doubt. But I say the defense has proven its case beyond a reasonable doubt and the District Attorney's case has not a leg to stand on. Now I will proceed to examine the evidence submitted by the District Attorney and let you see what he has proven and how he has proven it.

His case was so "strong" that he had immediately to lay his strongest proof before you by producing here a printer and a bookbinder, an expressman and a telephone man. And he actually proved, gentlemen of the jury, that MOTHER EARTH was printed at a printer's. He actually proved that THE BLAST was bound in a bindery. He proved that an expressman actually delivered packages of MOTHER EARTH to the MOTHER EARTH office. He proved that packages of THE BLAST were delivered to THE BLAST office. Do you think a paper is printed without a printer, without an electrotyper to make electros from the pictures and illustrations? Do you think we do not need an expressman to deliver packages? Why did the District Attorney waste your time and patience by proving these things? Because he can prove nothing else. All those things were admitted by the defense. Ridiculous even to submit such things in evidence! And lo, and behold, we get a new Sherlock Holmes upon the scene, Harold A. Content! He discovers a tremendous secret and submits it to you as his chief piece of evidence. What is that big discovery of our great detective? The No-Conscription Manifesto, the No-Conscription Manifesto that was sent out in 50,000 copies all over the country. The No-Conscription Manifesto that was read by millions of people in this country. *Some* secret! By millions of people—because practically every big paper in New York and Chicago and in all the other cities reprinted the manifesto, some in whole, some in excerpts. Millions of people have read it. Fifty thousand copies were sent out through the mails of the Federal Government. It required this great Sherlock Holmes to discover to you the secret, the existence of a No-Conscription Manifesto. I think, gentlemen of the jury, the very fact that the District Attorney had to submit such inadequate, irrelevant, absolutely useless facts as proof is an insult to your intelligence as jurymen. And when we come to the No-Conscription Manifesto, what do you find there? The word registration is not even mentioned. And here is his own charge about registration. The whole charge, the indictment of conspiracy to induce people not to register is based practically on this manifesto; and this manifesto never mentions the word registration. Some detective. Some proof. Some foundation for this ridiculous charge! Now let me read to you just one more passage to tell you the real meaning of this manifesto. The No-Conscription Manifesto, the very title of it, No-Conscription, not "No-Registration." Do you think if I wanted a No-Registration pamphlet I would issue a No-Conscription pamphlet? Have I ever hidden my meaning? Have I not always been frank to express it and perfectly free to voice my views? Why, the very purpose of my work is to express my views. They say we published a No-Conscription Manifesto when we meant No-Registration—we who have been only too frank all through this trial; who mean to be frank the rest of our lives; who have been frank all through the past, beginning with Russia, and suffered for it, too. We have said No-Conscription when we meant No-Registration! And what does this No-Conscription Manifesto say, in essence? "Liberty of conscience is the most fundamental of all human rights, the pivot of all progress. No man may be deprived of it without losing every vestige of freedom of thought and action. In these days when every principle and conception of democracy and of liberty is being cast overboard under the pretext of democratizing Germany, it behooves every liberty-loving man and woman to insist on his or her right of individual choice in the ordering of his life and actions." And here is again a passage that gives the very gist of the matter in one sentence: "The No-Conscription League is to be the voice of protest against the coercion of conscientious objectors to participate in the war." The gist of the No-Conscription movement in one paragraph. The No-Conscription movement is for the purpose of giving voice to protest, expressing the opinions of the conscientious objectors who do not want to participate in the war. That was the purpose of the No-Conscription movement. That was the purpose of the No-Conscription manifesto. Here it is expressed in the plainest, simplest language. And only a District Attorney could misunderstand it or try to delude you with the claim that the manifesto referred to No-Registration instead of dealing, as it does, exclusively with Conscription. It was necessary for the District Attorney to resort to such cheap subterfuge to bolster up the preposterous position of the Government in regard to the charge against us.

There were four No-Conscription mass meetings addressed by Miss Goldman. You will remember that the first No-Conscription meeting took place in Harlem River Casino, on May 18th. The next meeting of the League was held in Hunts' Point Palace, June 4th. Another meeting in Forward Hall, on June 14th. That is three meetings. Miss Goldman had also spoken, by invitation of another organization, in Royal Lyceum, June 11th. That is also in the evidence. Four meetings in all. Three of them were addressed also by me. What has the District Attorney produced with regard to those meetings? He has concentrated all his evidence on the meeting of May 18th. Now, gentlemen of the jury, it may not be quite clear to you why he did so. But there was a good reason, and no one knows the reason better than the defendants and Mr. District Attorney. There was a strong reason for centering the attention of the jury on the meeting of May 18th, and practically ignoring the speeches made at the other meetings. I will tell you the secret, and I want you to listen carefully. The District Attorney knew, and we can prove it, that we had our own stenographic notes of the meetings of June 4 and 14. The only meeting of which we did not have stenographic notes was the meeting of May 18th. The District Attorney selects May 18th. He knew that we had an expert shorthand reporter, engaged by the S. S. Corporation, take notes of the June 4 and June 14 speeches. The only meeting we had no notes of was that of May 18th. The District Attorney used the May 18th meeting as his chief argument. I will show you a moment later how he used those notes. But bear in mind just now that that is the only meeting of which we had no stenographic notes, and that the prosecution knew this fact.

In the first place, I hold that the meeting of May 18th had no business to be in this evidence at all. Not that we are not willing to stand for anything we have said. We have made it a principle of our lives to accept responsibility for articles in our magazines of which we do not even approve. We have stated on previous occasions, and I want to repeat now, that we are prepared to stand responsible for any article that ever appeared in MOTHER EARTH or in THE BLAST—no matter who wrote it, no matter whether the author is dead or alive, no matter what he says there, no matter even if I am entirely opposed to what he says. Why? Because we believe in free speech, and MOTHER EARTH was esablished just for that purpose. THE BLAST was established for the purpose of giving workingmen a chance to say what they think. We believe in free speech, and that is why you will find various, and sometimes contradictory, opinions expressed in MOTHER EARTH as well as in THE BLAST.

What I want to point out to you now, gentlemen, is that the meeting of May 18th had no business in this evidence. The District Attorney is a lawyer, a learned lawyer, and he knew it had no business in this case at all. Why did it have no business? Because the meeting of May 18th, according to the prosecution's own testimony, took place before there was such a thing in this country as a conscription law. We are indicted under the conscription—

THE COURT: Mr. Berkman, I do not want you to lose any unnecessary time on that subject. The Court is going to charge the jury that the Selective Service Law went into effect on the 18th day of May.

ALEXANDER BERKMAN: Very well.

THE COURT: And that at the time the meeting was held it was the duty of all persons not to violate the statute. The Court is going to charge that as a matter of law.

ALEXANDER BERKMAN: I am glad that the Court supports my contention that the Conscription Bill was not signed until May 18th. And I want to point out to you that it was signed by the President of the United States at ten o'clock at night, May 18th. The witness of the District Attorney stated here that Miss Goldman spoke on May 18th at 9:15 P. M., and that her speech was finished at 9.45. Besides that, gentlemen of the jury, you know what meetings are. Miss Goldman and I, being at a mass meeting, how could we know whether the President signed the bill or not? I do not want to argue along this line. I merely point out to you the character of this testimony, the spirit of this persecution—not prosecution—and the motive back of it, to which I will come later.

Now, then, the meeting of May 18th, and that particular speech quoted, took place before the Conscription Bill became a law or had the signature of the President. Gentlemen, there is another important point about the meeting of May 18th. The District Attorney found himself in a dilemma. It was hard for him to decide what should be done about these meetings, and especially the meeting of May 18th. You will see in a moment how he solved his dilemma. The May 18th meeting was the result of a wide-spread agitation that went on all over the country, because conscription was then discussed in Congress. The question of conscription was being agitated throughout the country. Many Congressmen voiced their constitutional objections and reasons against conscription. Many of them argued that it is contrary to the best interests of the country, contrary to the traditions of America, contrary to the very spirit of liberty upon which this republic is supposed to have been founded. There was a great deal of excitement in the country. Every person has a right to discuss. And naturally every one was very much interested. Mass meetings were taking place throughout the land, in opposition to conscription. One of them was the meeting of May 18th, at which Miss Goldman and myself spoke. Does it not appeal to your common sense that the chief topic of discussion at that meeting would be conscription? Registration was practically unknown then. The country hardly knew what registration was about, at that time. The Bill had not yet been signed, as I have called your attention to before. Conscription overshadowed every other issue on that day. Registration was not an issue. All the speeches at the meeting of May 18th were devoted, almost exclusively, to the discussion of conscription. Now, the District Attorney knew that. And there was his dilemma. What should he do to make the speech of Miss Goldman, on that particular evening, the most important link in his evidence? There was very little, perhaps nothing, about registration in her speech. Yet he had to make something of it. I will tell you what he did: he *doctored the document.*

I charge now and right here, and I am willing to take the consequences, that he doctored the stenographic notes of the patrolman with regard to the meeting of May 18th. And I am going to prove it to you right now. How did he doctor them? First of all, let us consider this wonderful stenographer who is really a patrolman, who has very little experience in stenography, as has been shown you, and who is only a third-grade stenographer, not an expert shorthand reporter. He could not tell you when he took stenographic notes previous to the meeting of May 18th. He stood there, confused, and when I asked him: "Tell us, when did you take stenographic notes before," he could not mention any occasion when he took stenographic notes at a meeting, except May 18th, Miss Goldman's speech. And then, gentlemen, when we put him to the test here, when Miss Goldman dictated to him in your own presence,—why, he dropped his hands at the second sentence: he could not take anything because he has no experience. And here this man, a patrolman, not really a stenographer, not a court reporter, who passed only with 125 or 120 words maximum, incompetent, by his own testimony—this third-grade, not third-grade really, but what in common language we would call tenth-grade stenographer—claims that he took down the total speech of Miss Goldman on May 18th! And how did he take it down? I am going to use his own testimony. He stood with both feet on a beer table, a round flat-topped beer table having only one leg; he stood in the center, people were passing up and down and jostling him, he was leaning against the wall with his hand in an insecure position, and thus he was taking down the speech of one of the fastest speakers in this country. Miss Goldman is considered the third fastest speaker in America, and only experts can take her speeches. Are you going to believe the testimony of this acrobatic stenographer? But Mr. Randolph, this patrolman who acts as a stenographer on one particular occasion in all his life, this Mr. Randolph has a very simple system. He just leaves out the words that he does not get. He leaves out the sentences he does not get, and he puts in the things he thinks should be there. That is his system, according to his own testimony, gentlemen. I do not want to say anything against Mr. Randolph personally. I am sorry for Randolph. He is not a bad man. He is just weak, and he is a patrolman. He may have a wife and family. He wants to keep his job. It is a tragedy, gentlemen, that a man has to keep his job by such methods. But it is not the fault of Mr. Randolph. Randolph has it in his stenographic notes that Miss Goldman said, "We believe in violence and we will use violence." That is the sentence he has and he sticks to that sentence. Now, of course, that is Mr. Randolph's idea of an Anarchist's speech. It had to be in. He was sent there to put that in. But maybe you, gentlemen, will have a different conception of Anarchist speeches before we are through. You have heard some Anarchist speeches delivered here, since you have been so patiently listening in this court for many days. You have heard Anarchist articles read. I want you to compare, in your own minds, the spirit and the manner of expression in the Anarchist speeches and articles you have heard here from the defendants with the spirit and the character of this would-be Anarchist expression, "We believe in violence and we will use violence."

Gentlemen, I don't think I need to waste much time in

proving to you that it was an impossibility for Miss Goldman to use such an expression. I challenge anyone, without the least fear of successful contradiction, to prove to me that in her twenty-seven years of experience on the public platform Miss Goldman ever used such an expression, or anything similar to such an expression, or anything that might be construed as meaning anything similar to that expression. Miss Goldman speaks about 250 times every year; she has lectured in practically every city and town; she has spoken to hundreds of thousands; in every city she has been welcomed again and again by the best minds. Do you mean to tell me that the incoherent thing that was read on the stand by the policeman can be credited to this intelligent woman? That incoherent, stupid, unconnected statement, that forgery—and a poor stupid forgery at that. Do you mean to tell me that that stuff is the speech of a trained, practiced orator like Miss Goldman? I leave it to your intelligence, gentlemen of the jury.

Nor is it necessary to dwell much upon the various pamphlets, leaflets and books written by Miss Goldman. Most of them are in evidence here. I haven't time to read them, nor do I wish to try your patience. But I challenge anyone, and the District Attorney especially, to pick out a single sentence in any of her books, in any of her pamphlets, that can even be interpreted as meaning what this patrolman-stenographer tells you, "We believe in violence and we will use violence." I have spoken to you before about the true meaning of Anarchism, and I don't think it is necessary to repeat that the very spirit and philosophy of Anarchism, for which we stand, proves that this document, this police stenographic report, is *inherently* false. Within itself it contains the proof that the expression attributed to Miss Goldman is not in harmony with her ideas and is, in fact, contrary to everything she has been advocating for many years.

I don't think I shall bother much more with the testimony of Mr. Randolph. I said that I am sorry for him, and now I am through with his evidence. But he was corroborated by another man, Edward Cadell, the acting detective. Now, what does Cadell say? Cadell swears that he took down every word, and he reads quoting allegedly what Miss Goldman said: "When they are conscripted they will not register." Such an idiotic statement! Does, then, conscription come first, registration afterwards? First they won't be conscripted, she says, according to Cadell, and then they will not register. That is the statement of your acting detective, as good a stenographer, every bit, as Mr. Randolph. Mr. Acting Detective also has another statement. He quotes Miss Goldman in a wonderful manner: "Breshnabotsky was tortured." I don't blame the witness for not being familiar with Russian history, or the history of the Russian Revolution and the names of our great martyrs. I don't blame him in the least. But I will point out something significant to you. I will point out to you that that sentence alone proves that this testimony was manufactured to order. It would have been absolutely impossible for Miss Goldman to say, "Breshnabotsky was tortured." In the first place, the name is Breshkovskaya. It is the name of the "Grandmother of the Russian Revolution," the woman who served forty years in Siberia, the noblest woman that the world has seen, with the exception of Miss Goldman; the woman who visited this country a few years ago, and was entertained and honored by the best representatives of American thought. Then she returned to Russia under the Czar, was arrested for her activities—the same activities that Miss Goldman has been following in this country; she was arrested and sent to Siberia again; a woman eighty years old. She is called the "Grandmother of the Russian Revolution." She was true to her ideals through long years in the mines of Kara, the mines where life is death; through all the years of her Siberian existence she has remained true to the ideals of Liberty, and she has now been called back by the triumphant Revolution of Russia to advise her people, to guide and enlighten them, to help them carry the banner of the Rusian Revolution into the open road of sunshine, of liberty and joy. That is Breshkovskaya. That is the woman to whom Miss Goldman referred, and I assure you there is no one in this country who is more familiar with the life and activities of Madame Breshkovskaya than Miss Goldman, because she is, as she has indeed been called, the Breshkovskaya of America. According to the police stenographer Miss Goldman said, "Breshkovskaya was tortured." Miss Goldman could not have said it. Breshkovskaya was never tortured. Miss Goldman knows it. What she did say was that Breshkovskaya has just been called back. She gave the story of Madame Breshkovskaya. She told about her exile—

THE COURT: Just a minute. There is no evidence to that effect.

ALEXANDER BERKMAN: That is where another sentence comes in—

THE COURT: Then read it. You cannot state any evidence that has not been introduced. You cannot make your own statements.

ALEXANDER BERKMAN: I am speaking of "Breshkovskaya tortured." The stenographer's words—

THE COURT: You can take the stenographer's words. You can read any part of it. But you cannot make a statement to the jury of what you heard or what the co-defendant heard or said, because no such evidence was introduced excepting by the witness. You can state anything the witness has said.

ALEXANDER BERKMAN: Very well. Gentlemen of the jury, I am referring—I am not a lawyer and don't know all these technical points; perhaps they are insignificant and not important—I am referring to those particular words "Breshkovskaya was tortured." It is a lie. Breshkovskaya never was tortured. Emma Goldman could not possibly say that Breshkovskaya was tortured, any more than you could say that President Wilson was a prisoner in Russia. She mentioned another woman who was tortured, Spiridonova—

MR. CONTENT: This is not evidence, your Honor.

ALEXANDER BERKMAN: I can't be interferred with every moment.

THE COURT: Just one moment; you will be interefered with when you do not follow the rules applicable in court. You cannot state anything that is not in evidence. You cannot state to this jury unsworn and not subject to cross-examination any interpretation of yours of what took place. You can have the fullest opportunity with the greatest latitude to discuss the evidence produced on this witness stand, whether that evidence was the evidence of the two stenographers who are members of the Police Department or was the evidence of witnesses produced by either the prosecution or the defendants. The jury is instructed to utterly disregard any statement made by either of the defendants or by the District Attorney which is not in evidence.

ALEXANDER BERKMAN: Gentlemen of the jury, it is sufficient to establish here the fact that Miss Goldman could not possibly have said Breshkovskaya was tortured; and that is all that is necessary to say about that part of the evidence of the man who corroborated Mr. Randolph, and who is an acting detective.

I want to say this here: That not having been trained to talk to a jury, and this being my first experience, it is rather confusing to be interrupted. Now, gentlemen, the fact is that neither Randolph nor the witness who corroborated him could take Miss Goldman's speech. She speaks too rapidly. You heard the testimony of two of the best experts in this country, one of whom was at one time the champion in his line. You heard his testimony that Miss Goldman frequently at meetings and lectures speaks two hundred words a minute, and that she is the third fastest speaker in the country. And that will explain, I think, why there are such nonsensical statements in the stenographic notes of the police transcript of the May 18th meeting, and why there are statements that are inherently false, statements that could not possibly have been made by Miss Goldman. You have also heard another expert shorthand reporter; I believe his name is Mr. Pickler. He was put on as a witness by the prosecution. He is the expert shorthand reporter of the S. S. Corporation which engaged him to take down the speeches. Mr. Pickler testified that he had never met either Miss Goldman or myself, until the meeting of May 18th. He is the witness of the prosecution. But the spirit of the prosecution is evidenced when it shouts at its own witness, "You are prejudiced in favor of the defense!" Of course, in the opinion of the District Attorney, any witness who tells the truth on the stand necessarily must be prejudiced in favor of the defense. Mr. Pickler does not know us and is not in sympathy with our ideas. But you looked at him, and I am sure you have never seen a finer type of American—an open, frank face, an honest expression, the very personification of frankness. The District Attorney tries to discredit his own witness, and fails miserably.

Now, gentlemen of the jury, I pride myself, justly or wrongly, on being a bit of a psychologist, and I divide the witnesses of the prosecution in classes, just to save time, instead of analyzing their testimony one by one. I can safely divide the witnesses of the prosecution into three classes. One class consisted of witnesses who gave entirely immaterial testimony. It is detective Barnitz, Officer McGee, the telephone man, the expressman, and a few more. I want to say that Detective Barnitz told nothing but the truth. He testified to our arrest: that we were frank about our work; that we did not try to resist, and so forth. Officer McGee testified that he confiscated certain documents. I say that these witnesses were of the first class, whose testimony is entirely immaterial with regard to the real charge at issue, the conspiracy to urge people not to register.

The second class comprised the printer of the Grayzel Press, the printer of the Graphic Press, the manager of the Harlem River Casino, where the meeting was held on May 18th, Mr. Wood, the binder, and several others. The evidence given by this class of witnesses was entirely in favor of the defense. You have heard what Mr. Wood said about Miss Goldman; how he respects and admires her. You have heard what the other witnesses testified to about the friendly relations we have had with all these business men. That is all there was to this testimony. You have also heard the testimony of Mr. Michael who owns, or rather pays rent for, the front room at 20 East 125th Street, third floor, and who was good enough to let us use his room for a while. You listened to the testimony of Mr. Kelly. All of them belong to the same class of witnesses, some for the prosecution, some for the defense, all testifying to immaterial facts, merely showing that there were our offices, that our relations were friendly, that our work was no secret, that MOTHER EARTH has been in existence for twelve years and that it passed through the Post Office as second class mail matter. Also that THE BLAST had an office on the third floor, back, in the same building as MOTHER EARTH, and that everything was done openly and above board in the frankest manner. That is the testimony of the first and the second class witnesses.

Now we come to the witnesses of the third class: the patrolman who wants to be a stenographer, and the stenographer who is an active detective. Then several Federal men, a soldier, and so forth. All interested and prejudiced witnesses, gentlemen; witnesses who do not like us, who do not understand us, who have no conception of our ideals, and by whom we have been misrepresented. But even they—what do they prove? Absolutely nothing. Even with all these witnesses, with the whole power of the Federal Government back of him, with the machinery of the Police Department and the detective bureau of the City of New York—with all this tremendous power back of the District Attorney, what did he prove against us? Nothing, absolutely nothing, except what we ourselves cheerfully and proudly admitted.

Now, gentlemen, as to the conspiracy itself, I think it would be ridiculous to dwell upon it. You have had us before your eyes for about ten or more days. You have heard us, you have had an opportunity to study our characters. I leave it to your own intelligence to judge whether we are the kind that slink about, that conspire in dark corners, that hide; whether we are the sort of people that make conspiracies,—unless our friendship and comradeship for the last twenty-seven or thirty years can be considered a conspiracy, the friendship and comradeship of which I am proud. Gentlemen, as to a conspiracy, there ain't no such animal in this zoo!

As impossible as it was for the District Attorney to prove a conspiracy, impossible because it did not exist, just as unsuccessful was he in proving any overt acts. Perhaps if I were a lawyer I would stop right here, because since he did not prove any conspiracy the whole charge falls; and even if there had been any overt acts the charge falls, because we are indicted for conspiracy and I have proven, I think, and I believe the intelligence of the jurors themselves will convince them, that the very suggestion of a conspiracy is ridiculous, preposterous, taking into consideration the facts of the situation and the character of the work we have been doing for the past thirty years. The conspiracy has not been proven—but I am not satisfied merely to show you that the District Attorney failed to prove his case. I want to demonstrate to you that the defendants *did* prove their case beyond a reasonable doubt. They are not expected to do so. But I shall not be satisfied in my own conscience until I show that to you. I know I can. I say that the District Attorney proved neither conspiracy nor any overt acts in furtherance of any imaginary conspiracy. Now, what are the overt acts that he is charging us with?

He talks about the May 18th meeting. Miss Goldman and

I had a conspiracy there, he says, and he quotes her alleged speech. But why didn't he quote anything from my speech?

I am supposed to have entered into a conspiracy with Miss Goldman. She makes a speech, according to the District Attorney, and I, the co-conspirator, do not even say a word in furtherance of my conspiracy. Not a word quoted from my speech, my great conspiratory speech of May 18th! The District Attorney did read my speech of June 4th, and not a line in it about any conspiracy or urging against registration. So it seems that we had a conspiracy, but one of the two conspirators never said a word in furtherance of his conspiracy. There were meetings, and there were speeches, and Mr. District Attorney has those speeches, and the co-conspirator Alexander Berkman never uttered a word to further the conspiracy. If we had really had a conspiracy, it would be insulting to me to be proven such a poor conspirator.

What are the other proofs of the prosecution that show us guilty of overt acts in furtherance of the conspiracy? There is nothing of any proof in the falsified notes of the stenographer. Suppose I admit, just for the sake of the argument, that what Randolph took down, "We believe in violence and we will use it," is correct. Where is the conspiracy, and where is the urging not to register? What has that to do with any conspiracy? Why, the detectives, numbers of them, were at the meeting; representatives of the Marshal's office, Federal officers, soldiers and everybody else were present. Miss Goldman is supposed to have said, "We will use violence," and nobody arrests her. She is not arrested for inciting to riot when all those officials of the City, State and Federal Government hear her say, "We believe in violence and we will use violence." Why was she not arrested? Because she did not utter those words. You can bet your life that she would have been arrested mighty quick if she had said anything like that. But I go further. Suppose she did say that. What has it to do with any conspiracy? Is she charged with inciting to riot? Is it charged that a riot took place? Why did they put in that sentence? Why is that sentence, that one sentence, the strongest link of the prosecution? Why put it in when it has nothing to do with the conspiracy against registration, absolutely nothing to do with urging people not to register? The answer is, because they had nothing else.

Now, what other alleged testimony or proof has been produced by the prosecution? The articles of MOTHER EARTH of the year 1914, articles dealing with reports of speeches held in Union Square under peculiar conditions, as the result of a special situation in the United States, at the time of the great miners' strike in Colorado. Mind you, speeches in 1914, by people, some of whom Miss Goldman probably does not even know. That is put in evidence as proving conspiracy under this new law of May 18, 1917. Is that evidence to prove that Miss Goldman urged people not to register on May 18, 1917? Have they submitted anything from MOTHER EARTH to connect us in any way with a conspiracy not to register? Have they produced any articles, old or new, that tell people "Do not register"? I am pointing out to you the character of this prosecution. I think you know, from your own impressions during the trial, that we stand for the things we believe in. If I wanted to say to people "Don't register," would I say to them, "I am opposed to conscription"? I am not that kind of a man. I *am* opposed to conscription, and I will say so. But if I wanted to urge people not to register, I would not tell them that I am opposed to conscription: I would tell them not to register. I demand that the District Attorney show evidence to the effect that either I or Miss Goldman advised any one not to register, or ever said in our speeches, or in MOTHER EARTH or in THE BLAST, "Don't register," or "You should not register." We are accustomed to say what we feel like saying, what we believe is right for us to say. Don't try to misinterpret the meaning of words. Words have their particular meaning, gentlemen of the jury, and even if I have to say it myself, I think I can use words in their proper meaning. I think I am an accurate writer. In fact, I am more accurate as a writer than as a speaker. I do not pretend to be an orator. I am now uttering what I consider common sense, as man to man. In my writings I am particularly accurate. I should consider it an insult to me, as a literary man, if anyone tried to misinterpret the meaning of my words, if anyone tried to tell me: "You meant a different thing when you said this. You said this and you meant something else." I say what I mean, in public and in private. I have no double character. I have no private character. My public and my private character is the same. I will say here in the court room—as I said before and as I will continue to say as long as my voice holds out—just what I believe. It is not a question of public speeches, not a question of any mass meetings or writings in MOTHER EARTH or in THE BLAST. I have said, do say, and will say just what I believe. I do not want any other words put in my mouth, words I have not said, things I have not meant. I stand for everything published in MOTHER EARTH and in THE BLAST, because we believe in free speech: we believe that free speech is the very foundation of liberty in this country or in any other country. I believe that the moment you begin to limit free speech, the moment you begin to persecute those who believe in the use of free speech, that moment you are committing the worst crime against liberty, the worst crime against democracy, the worst crime against the traditions in which you believe, the worst crime against the best interests of the people, because the abolition of free speech is a bad thing, gentlemen. Free speech is a sacred thing. Russia knows it. All other countries know it. And you, gentlemen of the jury, are intelligent enough to know that this country was originally founded upon the liberty of conscience, upon free speech, upon the free expression and discussion of opinion. We may be wrong. May be Anarchism is all wrong. May be all our ideas are wrong. But I claim the right even to be wrong. I may express any opinion. If I am wrong, I am willing to discuss with you, willing to discuss with anyone. It was I who sent word to the soldiers that I believe in free speech and that I would therefore give them the platform, though we did not expect them. I believe free discussion and free speech should not be limited under any pretext. It is a dangerous thing to do. It is the assassination of liberty.

Suppose we are wrong. Suppose our ideas are wrong. Is that any reason why we are guilty of conspiracy on this charge? Is that a reason to believe that we conspired or told people not to register? Why, gentlemen of the jury, many of the idealists of the past were told that they were wrong, but history proved them right. What if we are not wrong, after all? If you try to suppress us, you rob the people of the opportunity to learn our ideas. If our views are foolish, no intelligent person will accept them. There is no danger in letting a man talk foolishly. But there may be danger for the monopolist and the speculator in human blood to let people tell the truth. There may be danger. Perhaps in this you will find the explanation why they try to suppress those who tell the truth. I must emphasize that. There is no danger in getting up here and expressing foolish ideas. I could not convert you, if my ideas are foolish. There would be no harm done. But if my ideas are right, you will commit the greatest mistake in suppressing their expression. And therefore I say that I believe in the right of being wrong, as much as in the right of being right. In short, I believe in complete free speech. I am willing to take the consequences that may follow from the expression of my opinions. That is free speech. And it is for that reason that you will find, for instance, in MOTHER EARTH or in THE BLAST articles that sometimes really contradict themselves. Why? Because we open our pages to everyone, believing in free expression and in the free discussion of all views. Out of such discussion, I am sure, and only out of such discussion, can there come clarity, come understanding, and that which is of the greatest benefit and blessing to humanity—sympathy.

I don't like to take up too much time, but the District Attorney has read here an article by Alexander Berkman, called "Registration," from the last issue of THE BLAST, June, 1917. I haven't time to read it all to you. You have heard it read before, and I just want to point out to you what spirit animated the interpretation of the prosecution. I said in that article that registration is the first step toward conscription. The District Attorney read that sentence in a very peculiar tone, calculated to insinuate into your minds something that was not in the article. I have said, and I repeat, that registration is the first step to conscription. But, gentlemen of the jury, is that equivalent to urging people not to register? If I say to you, "I have taken the first step into the restaurant," does it mean that I have urged *you* to eat? When I say that registration is the first step to conscription, I have stated what I consider to be a fact. But that does not mean that registration and conscription are synonymous. Everyone understands that registration is one thing, conscription another. The District Attorney tries to interpret that statement as meaning "Don't register." Now take the other sentence: "The consistent conscientious objector to human slaughter will neither register nor be conscripted," a statement which I believe is true, and which is an expression of my opinion. But since when is an expression of opinion to be considered as urging people to do or not to do a thing? Since when is opinion to be interpreted as an act? There is a very clear distinction, gentlemen of the jury. Don't let any technical legal point confuse you about such a simple matter. There is expression of opinion, and there are acts. No sane man will say that expression of an opinion is the same thing as an act, or that an expression of opinion means advice to others. Ridiculous! If I say to you "I am hungry," does it mean I urge you to eat? If I say that registration is the first step to conscription, does it mean that I tell you that you should not register?

Gentlemen, I have mentioned several times that I am opposed to war, to capitalist war, and that I believe in universal peace and the constructive tendencies of man. I believe that through education, through organization, through enlightenment we will bring people to the point of sanity where war will become impossible, where the destructive tendencies will disappear, and misery, desperation and poverty, the sources of crime, will be things of the past. I believe that with the whole power of my heart and mind. May be I shall not see that day in my own lifetime. But that makes no difference. I believe these things are absolutely true.

It has further been shown to you that we do not believe in conscription. I consider conscription the death-blow to American liberty, or to any other kind of liberty. I believe we are making ourselves the laughing stock of the world by claiming that we stand for liberty and democracy, while we force people to go to war when they don't believe in war. I am opposed to conscription. But I am not charged here with conspiracy against conscription. I am charged with conspiracy against registration, or rather conspiracy to urge men not to register. I believe that conscription is wrong. I believe that conscription is tyranny. I believe that if the people had more intelligence and courage, the law would never have been passed. It is an insult to the people of the United States, an insult to humanity, to say that you must go to war and slaughter, when you have conscientious objections to murder. We do not believe in that thing. According to your own conceptions, gentlemen, government derives its powers from the consent of the governed. The people of the United States have not been asked whether they want conscription. They have been dragged, they have been forced into conscription. And therefore I say that the people have the right to throw away what they do not want. They have the right either to repeal conscription or to resist conscription. Thomas Jefferson said that resistance to tyranny is the beginning of freedom. Thomas Jefferson, one of the greatest men you ever had in this country, said that it was not only the right of the people, but even their duty, to resist tyranny. Therefore we stated that we believe in resisting conscription, and we advised the people to organize mass meetings, to join their voice to our protest against militarism and thus help to arouse the public conscience.

Gentlemen of the jury, we Anarchists work to educate and enlighten. That is why we publish literature and seek to spread it. We have repeatedly emphasized our belief that, in proportion as the people become enlightened, they will abolish the evils with which society is festering to-day. We believe in education, and we have tried to inform the people about the menace of militarism, the criminality of war which is but murder. We held up to them the ideal toward which humanity should strive: the ideal of universal peace, brotherhood and labor solidarity. The District Attorney cast it up to us that we asked people to send money to us. We did. We need money to publish literature. The printer testified that he had to be paid.

Another article from THE BLAST was read to you by Prosecutor Content. I suppose District Attorneys are not supposed to be susceptible to humor. Content evidently did not know that it was a humorous sketch called "War Dictionary," by Alexander Berkman. Between ourselves, I rather prided myself on it, because it was the first time—so far as I know—that anyone thought of a war dictionary. One of the definitions reads: "The Allies, the fairies of Democracy." Fairies, you know, are supposed to bring you many blessings. But fairies are a myth. That is my idea of the Allies. They pretend to be fighting for liberty. England, especially, has promised all manner of good things to Ireland. But those promises are fairies: they will not materialize. My humorous definition of the Allies is one of the "strongest" links in the case of the prosecution.

Another definition is: "Free speech: say what you please, but keep your mouth shut." One more powerful proof in support of the conspiracy charge against us! But I shall not waste any more time analyzing such evidence. It would be an insult to your intelligence.

Now comes something with which I should have perhaps started my argument, and which is in itself sufficient proof that the alleged conspiracy did not exist, and that, furthermore, Miss Goldman had taken the very opposite attitude from what she is here charged with. I am referring to the statement Miss Goldman sent from Springfield, Massachusetts, to the No-Conscription meeting of May 23rd, regarding her position on registration. The District Attorney sneered when Miss Helen Boardman, Miss Fitzgerald and numerous other defense witnesses testified that they heard a statement read, a statement from Miss Goldman, at the May 23rd meeting. The District Attorney shouted, "I don't believe there was any such statement!" When I said that the document was among the effects confiscated in our office by the District Attorney, he jumped up and cried: "I will make you prove it." Well, we did prove it. The statement was found among the papers of the District Attorney. It is in evidence. It has been read to you, and you heard very clearly what Miss Goldman wrote: that she would refuse to advise young men not to register. That statement itself disproves the whole case of the prosecution.

In passing, I want to call your attention, gentlemen of the jury, to the type of witnesses produced by the prosecution, and those of the defense. On the one hand we have a soldier, who has made it his business to break up peace meetings and who is bitter against us. Then Federal officers, police and detectives, with a few other similar witnesses. For the defense there appeared men and women of the best calibre, such as Lincoln Steffens, Bolton Hall, Leonard Abbott, John Reed, Mrs. John Sloan, Miss Helen Boardman, Alter Brady, writer and poet, and a number of others, the flower of American manhood and womanhood. Did the District Attorney mean to tell you, as he sneered at them, that they all perjured themselves? For what? Some of them had never met us before. They testified they came to the meeting of May 18th, and to other meetings specially to see how far we "would go in breaking the law." They said they were disappointed. Some of them even came to the committee meetings of the No-Conscription League and to our offices to get advice about registration. They were disappointed because, as they themselves stated, we refused to advise them not to register. Miss Goldman's statement proves it, if any additional proof is necessary.

I will tell you why we refused to advise young men not to register.

I would never advise anyone to do a thing which does not endanger me. I am willing to resist tyranny. If I were willing and ready to resist tyranny, I might advise others to do so, because I myself would do it. I would be with them and take the responsibility. But I was excepted from that registration business. I did not have to register. I was beyond the age. I was not in danger. And would I advise anyone to do the thing which does not put me in danger? I would advise people once in a while, if I thought it necessary to do things, dangerous things; but I would be with them. Never would I advise anybody to do a thing that is dangerous and I not be there or I not be in danger. That is why I did not advise people not to register.

Gentlemen of the jury, I think that I should not use any more time with regard to the evidence. I believe it has been absolutely demonstrated here that the District Attorney has no case. He proved neither conspiracy nor any overt acts. It is further demonstrated that such a conspiracy could not possibly exist, and that all the previous acts of our enlightening propaganda and agitation and all the ideals of Miss Goldman and myself are inherently opposed to any such thing as a dark conspiracy, and that other circumstances which I have mentioned made it impossible for us to urge people not to register. I think I have sufficiently proven, beyond any reasonable doubt, that the defense or defendants never advised or urged anyone not to register and that there was no such conspiracy. I think I have said enough about that. If I argue this point, gentlemen, before I conclude, I want you to know that I am not arguing to keep myself from going to prison. I am not afraid of prison. I am willing to suffer for my ideas in prison, if necessary. Life is dear, but not so dear that I should be at liberty without self-respect. I would rather be in prison with my ideals, with my convictions, true to myself, than be outside with my soul damned in my own estimation. So I am not pleading to save ourselves from prison. Ourselves, I say, because I know that Miss Goldman shares my views and my feelings in this matter. No, it is not a question of prison with us. It is a question of whether we stand here indicted as guilty of conspiracy to induce people not to register, or whether the prosecution has tried to arouse your passions and prejudices against us as Anarchists. That is the question. It is really Anarchism that is on trial here, and I am glad it is, because it is well for you to know what Anarchism is, since we are Anarchists.

Gentlemen of the jury, this is an important, a solemn moment in your lives, in your lives much more than in mine. A solemn moment, because the eyes of the whole country, indeed the eyes of the world, are upon you. This is no petty question of telling some one not to register. The real question at issue here is, have we got free speech and liberty of expression in this country, or not. That is the real question, over and above this indictment, over and above all the fool things that have been said by the District Attorney. It is up to you, as representing, on this occasion, the American people, it is up to you as the jury in this case to tell the world by your verdict whether you believe that free speech is necessary and sacred, or whether you believe that your forefathers, the founders of this Republic, sacrificed their lives in vain, and that we should throw on the dungheap all those things for which they fought, for which people have bled, for which the martyrs of all countries have died: Free speech and liberty of expression and freedom of conscience. That is, that will be, the meaning of your verdict. It is not a question of a few years in prison. It is not a question of conspiracy or registration. Will you say by your verdict that people shall not talk in this country, that people shall not think, that people shall not dare express an opinion? And if you say "We have war," I say to you, because of the war it is necessary for you to show that we do have liberty, that we do have some democracy here. Why, yes, the war, you say, is for the very purpose of carrying democracy and liberty to Europe. Will you proclaim to the world that you who carry liberty and democracy to Europe have no liberty here, that you who are fighting for democracy in Germany, suppress democracy right here in New York, in the United States? Are you going to suppress free speech and liberty in this country, and still pretend that you love liberty so much that you will fight for it five thousand miles away? Charity begins at home, gentlemen of the jury. Liberty begins at home. That is where you begin right now, to-day, to show that you stand for liberty. *We* have spoken for liberty all our lives. Now *you* are put to the test as men who believe in liberty; you are put to the test. It is for you to show whether you believe in liberty. And let me tell you, whether you think that we are right or whether we are wrong, one thing you know: the spirit that animates this woman, the spirit that animates these defendants, is the spirit that has in the past emancipated the bondman. It is the spirit that will in the future emancipate the slave from his slavery, the tyrant from his tyranny; the spirit that will abolish war, make us all brothers of one family, without the evils and crimes that darken the world to-day, without oppression and monopoly, and make the world a fit place to live in, with a real motto, actually applied: Liberty for all, well-being for every one, and happiness for humanity.

Emma Goldman's Address to the Jury

GENTLEMEN OF THE JURY:

As in the case of my co-defendant, Alexander Berkman, this is also the first time in my life I have ever addressed a jury. I once had occasion to speak to three judges.

On the day after our arrest it was given out by the U. S. Marshal and the District Attorney's office that the "big fish" of the No-Conscription activities had been caught, and that there would be no more trouble-makers and disturbers to interfere with the highly democratic effort of the Government to conscript its young manhood for the European slaughter. What a pity that the faithful servants of the Government, personified in the U. S. Marshal and the District Attorney, should have used such a weak and flimsy net for their big catch. The moment the anglers pulled their heavily laden net ashore, it broke, and all the labor was so much wasted energy.

The methods employed by Marshal McCarthy and his hosts of heroic warriors were sensational enough to satisfy the famous circus men, Barnum & Baily. A dozen or more heroes dashing up two flights of stairs, prepared to stake their lives for their country, only to discover the two dangerous disturbers and trouble-makers, Alexander Berkman and Emma Goldman, in their separate offices, quietly at work at their desks, wielding not a sword, nor a gun or a bomb, but merely their pens! Verily, it required courage to catch such big fish.

To be sure, two officers equipped with a warrant would have sufficed to carry out the business of arresting the defendants Alexander Berkman and Emma Goldman. Even the police know that neither of them is in the habit of running away or hiding under the bed. But the farce-comedy had to be properly staged if the Marshal and the District Attorney were to earn immortality. Hence the sensational arrest; hence, also, the raid upon the offices of THE BLAST, MOTHER EARTH and the No-Conscription League.

In their zeal to save the country from the trouble-makers, the Marshal and his helpers did not even consider it necessary to produce a search warrant. After all, what matters a mere scrap of paper when one is called upon to raid the offices of Anarchists! Of what consequence is the sanctity of property, the right of privacy, to officials in their dealings with Anarchists! In our day of military training for battle, an Anarchist office is an appropriate camping ground. Would the gentlemen who came with Marshal McCarthy have dared to go into the offices of Morgan, or Rockefeller, or of any of those men without a search warrant? They never showed us the search warrant, although we asked them for it. Nevertheless,

EMMA GOLDMAN

they turned our office into a battlefield, so that when they were through with it, it looked like invaded Belgium, with the only difference that the invaders were not Prussian barbarians but good American patriots bent on making New York safe for democracy.

The stage having been appropriately set for the three-act comedy, and the first act successfully played by carrying off the villains in a madly dashing automobile—which broke every traffic regulation and barely escaped crushing every one in its way—the second act proved even more ludicrous. Fifty thousand dollars bail was demanded, and real estate refused when offered by a man whose property is rated at three hundred thousand dollars, and that after the District Attorney had considered and, in fact, promised to accept the property for one of the defendants, Alexander Berkman, thus breaking every right guaranteed even to the most heinous criminal.

Finally the third act, played by the Government in this court during the last week. The pity of it is that the prosecution knows so little of dramatic construction, else it would have equipped itself with better dramatic material to sustain the continuity of the play. As it was, the third act fell flat, utterly, and presents the question, Why such a tempest in a teapot?

Gentlemen of the jury, my comrade and co-defendant having carefully and thoroughly gone into the evidence presented by the prosecution, and having demonstrated its entire failure to prove the charge of conspiracy or any overt acts to carry out that conspiracy, I shall not impose upon your patience by going over the same ground, except to emphasize a few points. To charge people with having conspired to do something which they have been engaged in doing most of their lives, namely their campaign against war, militarism and conscription as contrary to the best interests of humanity, is an insult to human intelligence.

And how was that charge proven? By the fact that MOTHER EARTH and THE BLAST were printed by the same printer and bound in the same bindery. By the further evidence that the same expressman had delivered the two publications! And by the still more illuminating fact that on June 2nd MOTHER EARTH and THE BLAST were given to a reporter at his request, if your please, and gratis.

Gentlemen of the jury, you saw the reporter who testified to this overt act. Did any one of you receive the impression that the man was of conscriptable age, and if not, in what possible way is the giving of MOTHER EARTH to a reporter for news purposes proof demonstrating the overt act?

It was brought out by our witnesses that the MOTHER EARTH magazine has been published for twelve years; that it was never held up, and that it has always gone through the U. S. mail as second-class mail matter. It was further proven that the magazine appeared each month about the first or second, and that it was sold or given away at the office to whoever wanted a copy. Where, then, is the overt act?

Just as the prosecution has utterly failed to prove the charge of conspiracy, so has it also failed to prove the overt act by the flimsy testimony that MOTHER EARTH was given to a reporter. The same holds good regarding THE BLAST.

Gentlemen of the jury, the District Attorney must have learned from the reporters the gist of the numerous interviews which they had with us. Why did he not examine them as to whether or not we had counseled young men not to register? That would have been a more direct way of getting at the facts. In the case of the reporter from the New York *Times,* there can be no doubt that the man would have been only too happy to accommodate the District Attorney with the required information. A man who disregards every principle of decency and ethics of his profession as a newspaper man, by turning material given him as news over to the District Attorney, would have been glad to oblige a friend. Why did Mr. Content neglect such a golden opportunity? Was it not because the reporter of the *Times,* like all the other reporters, must have told the District Attorney that the two defendants stated, on each and every occasion, they would not tell people not to register?

Perhaps the *Times* reporter refused to go to the extent of perjuring himself. Patrolmen and detectives are not so timid in such matters. Hence Mr. Randolph and Mr. Cadell, to rescue the situation. Imagine employing tenth-rate stenographers to report the very important speeches of dangerous trouble-makers! What lack of forethought and efficiency on the part of the District Attorney! But even these two members of the police department failed to prove by their notes that we advised people not to register. But since they had to produce something incriminating against Anarchists, they conveniently resorted to the old standby, always credited to us, "We believe in violence and we will use violence."

Assuming, gentlemen of the jury, that this sentence was really used at the meeting of May 18th, it would still fail to prove the indictment which charges conspiracy and overt acts to carry out the conspiracy. And that is all we are charged with. Not violence, not Anarchism. I will go further and say, that had the indictment been for the advocacy of violence, you gentlemen of the jury, would still have to render a verdict of "Not Guilty," since the mere belief in a thing or even the announcement that you would carry out that belief, can not possibly constitute a crime.

However, I wish to say emphatically that no such expression as "We believe in violence and we will use violence" was uttered at the meeting of May 18th, or at any other meeting.

I could not have employed such a phrase, as there was no occasion for it. If for no other reason, it is because I want my lectures and speeches to be coherent and logical. The sentence credited to me is neither.

I have read to you my position toward political violence from a lengthy essay called "The Psychology of Political Violence."

But to make that position clearer and simpler, I wish to say that I am a social student. It is my mission in life to ascertain the cause of our social evils and of our social difficulties. As a student of social wrongs it is my aim to diagnose a wrong. To simply condemn the man who has committed an act of political violence, in order to save my skin, would be as unpardonable as it would be on the part of the physician, who is called to diagnose a case, to condemn the patient because the patient has tuberculosis, cancer, or some other disease. The honest, earnest, sincere physician does not only prescribe medicine, he tries to find out the cause of the disease. And if the patient is at all capable as to means, the doctor will say to him, "Get out of this putrid air, get out of the factory, get out of the place where your lungs are being infected." He will not merely give him medicine. He will tell him the cause of the disease. And that is precisely my position in regard to acts of violence. That is what I have said on every platform. I have attempted to explain the cause and the reason for acts of political violence.

It is organized violence on top which creates individual violence at the bottom. It is the accumulated indignation against organized wrong, organized crime, organized injustice which drives the political offender to his act. To condemn him means to be blind to the causes which make him. I can no more do it, nor have I the right to, than the physician who were to condemn the patient for his disease. You and I and all of us who remain indifferent to the crimes of poverty, of war, of human degradation, are equally responsible for the act committed by the political offender. May I therefore be permitted to say, in the words of a great teacher: "He who is without sin among you, let him cast the first stone." Does that mean advocating violence? You might as well accuse Jesus of advocating prostitution, because He took the part of the prostitute, Mary Magdalene.

Gentlemen of the jury, the meeting of the 18th of May was called primarily for the purpose of voicing the position of the conscientious objector and to point out the evils of conscription. Now, who and what is the conscientious objector? Is he really a shirker, a slacker, or a coward? To call him that is to be guilty of dense ignorance of the forces which impel men and women to stand out against the whole world like a glittering lone star upon a dark horizon. The conscientious objector is impelled by what President Wilson in his speech of Feb. 3, 1917, called "the righteous passion for justice upon which all war, all structure of family, State and of mankind must rest as the ultimate base of our existence and our liberty." The righteous passion for justice which can never express itself in human slaughter—that is the force which makes the conscientious objector. Poor indeed is the country which fails to recognize the importance of that new type of humanity as the "ultimate base of our existence and liberty." It will find itself barren of that which makes for character and quality in its people.

The meeting of May 18th was held before the Draft Bill had actually gone into effect. The President signed it late in the evening of the 18th. Whatever was said at that meeting, even if I had counseled young men not to register, that meeting cannot serve as proof of an overt act. Why, then, has the Prosecuting Attorney dwelt so much, at such length, and with such pains on that meeting, and so little on the other meetings held on the eve of registration and after? Is it not because the District Attorney knew that we had no stenographic notes of that meeting? He knew it because he was approached by Mr. Weinberger and other friends for a copy of the transcript, which request he refused. Evidently, the District Attorney felt safe to use the notes of a patrolman and a detective, knowing that they would swear to anything their superiors wanted. I never like to accuse anyone—I wouldn't go so far as my co-defendant, Mr. Berkman, in saying that the District Attorney doctored the document; I don't know whether he did or not. But I do know that Patrolman Randolph and Detective Cadell doctored the notes, for the simple reason that I didn't say those things. But though we could not produce our own stenographic notes, we have been able to prove by men and women of unimpeachable character and high intelligence that the notes of Randolph are utterly false. We have also proven beyond a reasonable doubt, and Mr. Content did not dare question our proof, that at the Hunts' Point Palace, held on the eve of registration, I expressly stated that I cannot and will not tell people not to register. We have further proven that this was my definite stand, which was explained in my statement sent from Springfield and read at the meeting of May 23rd.

When we go through the entire testimony given on behalf of the prosecution, I insist that there is not one single point to sustain the indictment for conspiracy or to prove the overt acts we are supposed to have committed. But we were even compelled to bring a man eighty years of age to the witness stand in order to stop, if possible, any intention to drag in the question of German money. It is true, and I appreciate it, that Mr. Content said he had no knowledge of it. But, gentlemen of the jury, somebody from the District Attorney's office or someone from the Marshal's office must have given out the statement that a bank receipt for $2,400 was found in my office and must have told the newspapers the fake story of German money. As if we would ever touch German money, or Russian money, or American money coming from the ruling class, to advance our ideas! But in order to forestall any suspicion, any insinuation, in order to stand clear before you, we were compelled to bring an old man here to inform you that he has been a radical all his life, that he is interested in our ideas, and that he is the man who contributed the money for radical purposes and for the work of Miss Goldman.

Gentlemen of the jury, you will be told by the Court, I am sure, that when you render a verdict you must be convinced beyond a reasonable doubt; that you must not assume that we are guilty before we are proven guilty; and that it is your duty to assume that we are innocent. And yet, as a matter of fact, the burden of proof has been laid upon us. We had to bring witnesses. If we had had time we could have brought fifty more witnesses, each corroborating the others. Some of those people have no relation with us. Some are writers, poets, contributors to the most conventional magazines. Is it likely that they would swear to something in our favor if it were not the truth? Therefore I insist, as did my co-defendant Alexander Berkman, that the prosecution has made a very poor showing in proving the conspiracy or any overt act.

Gentlemen of the jury, we have been in public life for twenty-seven years. We have been haled into court, in and out of season—we have never denied our position. Even the police know that Emma Goldman and Alexander Berkman are not shirkers. You have had occasion during this trial to convince yourselves that we do not deny. We have gladly and proudly claimed responsibility, not only for what we ourselves have said and written, but even for things written by others and with which we did not agree. Is it plausible, then, that we would go through the ordeal, trouble and expense of a lengthy trial to escape responsibility in this instance? A thousand times no! But we refuse to be tried on a trumped-up charge, or to be convicted by perjured testimony, merely because we are Anarchists and hated by the class whom we have openly fought for many years.

Gentlemen, during our examination of talesmen, when we asked whether you would be prejudiced against us if it were proven that we propagated ideas and opinions contrary to those held by the majority, you were instructed by the Court to say, "If they are within the law." But what the Court did not tell you is, that no new faith—not even the most humane and peaceable—has ever been considered "within the law" by those who were in power. The history of human growth is at the same time the history of every new idea heralding the approach of a brighter dawn, and the brighter dawn has always been considered illegal, outside of the law.

Gentlemen of the jury, most of you, I take it, are believers in the teachings of Jesus. Bear in mind that he was put to death by those who considered his views as being against the law. I also take it that you are proud of your Americanism. Remember that those who fought and bled for your liberties were in their time considered as being against the law, as dangerous disturbers and trouble-makers. They not only preached violence, but they carried out their ideas by throwing tea into the Boston harbor. They said that "Resistance to tyranny is obedience to God." They wrote a dangerous document called the Declaration of Independence. A document which continues to be dangerous to this day, and for the circulation of which a young man was sentenced to ninety days prison in a New York Court, only the other day. They were the Anarchists of *their* time—they were never within the law.

Your Government is allied with the French Republic. Need I call your attention to the historic fact that the great upheaval in France was brought about by extra-legal means? The Dantes, the Robespieres, the Marats, the Herberts, aye even the man who is responsible for the most stirring revolutionary music, the Marseillaise (which unfortunately has deteriorated into a war tune) even Camille Desmoulins, were never within the law. But for those great pioneers and rebels, France would have continued under the yoke of the idle Louis XVI., to whom the sport of shooting jack rabbits was more important than the destiny of the people of France.

Ah, gentlemen, on the very day when we were being tried for conspiracy and overt acts, your city officials and representatives welcomed with music and festivities the Russian Commission. Are you aware of the fact that nearly all of the members of that Commission have only recently been released from exile? The ideas they propagated were never within the law. For nearly a hundred years, from 1825 to 1917, the Tree of Liberty in Russia was watered by the blood of her martyrs. No greater heroism, no nobler lives had ever been dedicated to humanity. Not one of them worked within the law. I could continue to enumerate almost endlessly the hosts of men and women in every land and in every period whose ideas and ideals redeemed the world because they were not within the law.

Never can a new idea move within the law. It matters not whether that idea pertains to political and social changes or to any other domain of human thought and expression—to science, literature, music; in fact, everything that makes for freedom and joy and beauty must refuse to move within the law. How can it be otherwise? The law is stationary, fixed, mechanical, "a chariot wheel" which grinds all alike without regard to time, place and condition, without ever taking into account cause and effect, without ever going into the complexity of the human soul.

Progress knows nothing of fixity. It cannot be pressed into a definite mould. It cannot bow to the dictum, "I have ruled," "I am the regulating finger of God." Progress is ever renewing, ever becoming, ever changing—*never is it within the law.*

If that be crime, we are criminals even like Jesus, Socrates, Gallileo, Bruno, John Brown and scores of others. We are in good company, among those whom Havelock Ellis, the greatest living psychologist, describes as the political criminals recognized by the whole civilized world, except America, as men and women who out of deep love for humanity, out of a passionate reverence for liberty and an all-absorbing devotion to an ideal are ready to pay for their faith even with their blood. We cannot do otherwise if we are to be true to ourselves—we know that the political criminal is the precursor of human progress—the political criminal of to-day must needs be the hero, the martyr and the saint of the new age.

But, says the Prosecuting Attorney, the press and the unthinking rabble, in high and low station, "that is a dangerous doctrine and unpatriotic at this time." No doubt it is. But are we to be held responsible for something which is as unchangeable and unalienable as the very stars hanging in the heavens unto time and all eternity?

Gentlemen of the jury, we respect your patriotism. We would not, if we could, have you change its meaning for yourself. But may there not be different kinds of patriotism as there are different kinds of liberty? I for one cannot believe that love of one's country must needs consist in blindness to its social faults, to deafness to its social discords, of inarticulation to its social wrongs. Neither can I believe that the mere accident of birth in a certain country or the mere scrap of a citizen's paper constitutes the love of country.

I know many people—I am one of them—who were not born here, nor have they applied for citizenship, and who yet love America with deeper passion and greater intensity than many natives whose patriotism manifests itself by pulling, kicking, and insulting those who do not rise when the national anthem is played. Our patriotism is that of the man who loves a woman with open eyes. He is enchanted by her beauty, yet he sees her faults. So we, too, who know America, love her beauty, her richness, her great possibilities; we love her mountains, her canyons, her forests, her Niagara, and her deserts—above all do we love the people that have produced her wealth, her artists who have created beauty, her great apostles who dream and work for liberty—but with the same passionate emotion we hate her superficiality, her cant, her corruption, her mad, unscrupulous worship at the altar of the Golden Calf.

We say that if America has entered the war to make the world safe for democracy, she must first make democracy safe in America. How else is the world to take America seriously, when democracy at home is daily being outraged, free speech suppressed, peaceable assemblies broken up by overbearing and brutal gangsters in uniform; when free press is curtailed and every independent opinion gagged. Verily, poor as we are in democracy, how can we give of it to the world? We further say that a democracy conceived in the military servitude of the masses, in their economic enslavement, and nurtured in their tears and blood, is not democracy at all. It is despotism—the cumulative result of a chain of abuses which, according to that dangerous document, the Declaration of Independence, the people have the right to overthrow.

The District Attorney has dragged in our Manifesto, and he has emphasized the pasage, "Resist conscription." Gentlemen of the jury, please remember that that is not the charge against us. But admitting that the Manifesto contains the expression, "Resist conscription," may I ask you, is there only *one kind* of resistance? Is there only the resistance which means the gun, the bayonet, the bomb or flying machine? Is there not another kind of resistance? May not the people simply fold their hands and declare, "We will not fight when we do not believe in the necessity of war"? May not the people who believe in the repeal of the Conscription Law, because it is unconstitutional, express their opposition in word and by pen, in meetings and in other ways? What right has the District Attorney to interpret that particular passage to suit himself? Moreover, gentlemen of the jury, I insist that the indictment against us does not refer to conscription. We are charged with a conspiracy against registration. And in no way or manner has the prosecution proven that we are guilty of conspiracy or that we have committed an overt act.

Gentlemen of the jury, you are not called upon to accept our views, to approve of them or to justify them. You are not even called upon to decide whether our views are within or against the law. You are called upon to decide whether the prosecution has proven that the defendants Emma Goldman and Alexander Berkman have conspired to urge people not to register. And whether their speeches and writings represent overt acts.

Whatever your verdict, gentlemen, it cannot possibly affect the rising tide of discontent in this country against war which, despite all boasts, is a war for conquest and military power. Neither can it affect the ever increasing opposition to conscription which is a military and industrial yoke placed upon the necks of the American people. Least of all will your verdict affect those to whom human life is sacred, and who will not become a party to the world slaughter. Your verdict can only add to the opinion of the world as to whether or not justice and liberty are a living force in this country or a mere shadow of the past.

Your verdict may, of course, affect us temporarily, in a physical sense—it can have no effect whatever upon our spirit. For even if we were convicted and found guilty and the penalty were that we be placed against a wall and shot dead, I should nevertheless cry out with the great Luther: "Here I am and here I stand and I cannot do otherwise."

And gentlemen, in conclusion let me tell you that my codefendant, Mr. Berkman, was right when he said the eyes of America are upon you. They are upon you not because of sympathy for us or agreement with Anarchism. They are upon you because it must be decided sooner or later whether we are justified in telling people that we will give them democracy in Europe, when we have no democracy here? Shall free speech and free assemblage, shall criticism and opinion—which even the espionage bill did not include—be destroyed? Shall it be a shadow of the past, the great historic American past? Shall it be trampled underfoot by any detective, or policeman, anyone who decides upon it? Or shall free speech and free press and free assemblage continue to be the heritage of the American pople?

Gentlemen of the jury, whatever your verdict will be, as far as we are concerned, nothing will be changed. I have held ideas all my life. I have publicly held my ideas for twenty-seven years. Nothing on earth would ever make me change my ideas except one thing; and that is, if you will prove to me that our position is wrong, untenable, or lacking in historic fact. But never would I change my ideas because I am found guilty. I may remind you of two great Americans, undoubtedly not unkonwn to you, gentlemen of the jury; Ralph Waldo Emerson and Henry David Thoreau. When Thoreau was placed in prison for refusing to pay taxes, he was visited by Ralph Waldo Emerson and Emerson said: "David, what are you doing in jail?" and Thoreau replied: "Ralph, what are you doing outside, when honest people are in jail for their ideals?" Gentlemen of the jury, I do not wish to influence you. I do not wish to appeal to your passions. I do not wish to influence you by the fact that I am a woman. I have no such desires and no such designs. I take it that you are sincere enough and honest enough and brave enough to render a verdict according to your convictions, beyond the shadow of a reasonable doubt.

Please forget that we are Anarchists. Forget that it is

claimed that we propagated violence. Forget that something appeared in MOTHER EARTH when I was thousands of miles away, three years ago. Forget all that, and merely consider the evidence. Have we been engaged in a conspiracy? has that conspiracy been proven? have we committed overt acts? have those overt acts been proven? We for the defense say they have not been proven. And therefore your verdict must be not guilty.

But whatever your decision, the struggle must go on. We are but the atoms in the incessant human struggle towards the light that shines in the darkness—the Ideal of economic, political and spiritual liberation of mankind!

Address of Harold A. Content, Assistant United States Attorney, to the Jury

GENTLEMEN OF THE JURY:

Unfortunately I am sadly lacking in that eloquence of words that has distinguished Miss Goldman's oration. I am paid to talk for a living, but I am sure that if Miss Goldman wanted to accept a position in the Government service she could secure the finest kind of position by reason of her oratorical gifts. But perhaps I have something in the nature of a confession to make to you, because there was a time in my youthful career when I offered myself as a candidate for the State legislature, and I told with all my sincerity the voters in my district why they should vote for me, and you can judge the degree of success I had, when I tell you that I failed to be elected. But I feel in this case, that whereas the Government forces may not be able to place before you that eloquence, that impassioned oratory, that use of words that has so distinguished Miss Goldman during the past twenty or thirty years, still on the other hand the Government has brought before you an eloquence of facts that cannot be disregarded by any juror who is conscientiously trying to decide a question of fact upon the evidence submitted to him and upon nothing else. Now, gentlemen of the jury, you were told somewhat in the opening speech to the jury just what the law in question was.

(The Prosecutor here again defined the charge of conspiracy, the meaning of overt acts and reviewed the evidence.)

And now, gentlemen of the jury, before I pass to the other witnesses I just want to refer to a few things that were brought out in the summation of the defendants, that I haven't really thought of specially when I prepared these few remarks that I am giving you. Mr. Berkman among other things tried to give you a definition of an Anarchist. You, gentlemen, I assume, don't speak Greek. But he gave you an incorrect translation of the word "Anarche." The word "arche" means government. It does not mean violence. That is not the interpretation. So that the word "Anarchy" instead of meaning "without violence," means "absence, abolition of government," or "chaos," every man to do as he feels like, without regard to the rights of his neighbor, without regard to law and order. That's the true translation of the Greek word "anarche." So, don't be deluded by their contention that government is violence, and that any effort to do away with government is not violence, but is something that is done to destroy violence. That is their philosophy. And you had a very excellent sample of it when Mr. Abbott was on the stand and was inquired of as to the tenets of the Ferrer School in New York

City. I didn't bring that out. You gentlemen recall, all this talk about Mr. Francisco Ferrer was brought out over my objection. I had nothing to do with that. I didn't bring out that they were Anarchists. They brought that out themselves when they were examining talesmen. So that Mr. Abbott told you that this school of which he is the noble head, and of which these two defendants have the honor to be founders, teaches young people—think of it!—that they are above the law; teaches them what they call "self-reliance," that is to say, if you feel strong enough to defy a law of your country, why go ahead and defy it; only—be sure that you can get away with it. That is the doctrine of the Ferrer School. I didn't bring that out. They brought it out. And it is perhaps just as well for you, gentlemen, who doubtless have relatives in the public schools of this country, to know that and to consider how this country would succeed if doctrines of that sort were permitted to be promulgated among the young in this society.

Now, gentlemen of the jury, it is part of your province to pass upon the credibility of witnesses and I do not propose to take up your time by referring to each witness. But I shall do somewhat like my adversary. I shall break them off into groups. We first had Miss Fitzgerald who was called as a hostile witness. Miss Fitzgerald told you what the No-Conscription League was. She would not say in so many words that Mr. Berkman and Miss Goldman were prominent members of the league; she would only say that they were the ablest speakers. But what did we elicit from her? We elicited from her that the money with which the so-called league of Emma Goldman, Berkman & Company was run, was supplied by voluntary contributions, some of these contributions being taken up, as you can tell from the minutes read to you, at meetings where poor deluded people put in coppers and nickels and dimes, some as high as a dollar. And this money was taken, and what was done with it? It was placed to Alexander Berkman's credit in the account in his name. And you have in evidence a letter to the bank telling them to do it, and you have the further fact that on the bottom of the form letters contributors are asked to send the money to Berkman and Goldman for obvious reasons, not to the No-Conscription League. So what have you got? You have got the money that is taken for the avowed objects of this movement, put into the personal bank account of Alexander Berkman, mingled with other funds, funds from THE BLAST perhaps, funds perhaps from his writings, if there are any; and checks drawn in common on this fund, no accounting to anybody. If a trustee of any society in the State of New York handled accounts in that way he would be indicted for grand larceny and convicted. So as you examine Government's Exhibits 18 and 19 you have certain

Graphic Press bills and you have certain other payments, you have some money sent to Robert Minor for the San Francisco defense; and to be sure, they paid $25 deposit for the Hunts' Point Palace, and some other alleged bills. But you also have such significant items as a bill from a doctor who treated Mr. Berkman's foot.

Now gentlemen of the jury, you may say perhaps they had a right to support themselves because they were engaged in the work and didn't take any specific salary. But I call your attention to the fact that if Anarchy means that you can take poor people's money and mingle it with your own and give no accounting for it and use it for what you please including hotel checks, then I think a lot of us will be turning into Anarchists.

You had a lot of the gentlemen called who testified that they had known Mr. Berkman and Miss Goldman for a long while, that they were very ideal people and had never believed in violence and had always expressed themselves as opposed to violence. You had Mr. John Reed who got 30 days and doesn't know what for in Paterson, who told you in a very calm manner that God knows he was opposed to violence. And then you had Mr. Lincoln Steffens, and you had a psychological lady named Miss Boardman, if I recollect. And you had an Italian gentleman named Mr. Pietro Allegra who spoke at many meetings, and you had Mrs. Sloan, who had a very distinct recollection that Miss Goldman was unalterably opposed to violence. And you had a gentleman who formerly was a lawyer, but doesn't practice any more, Mr. Bolton Hall, who believes in free speech, whether it comes in conflict with the law or not, and he was sure that Miss Goldman was opposed to violence, although he once heard that she served time for unlawful assembly and inciting to riot. Now the theory of all these gentlemen was this: that she could not have used these words. The important part of that May 18th speech is not "We believe in violence and will use violence." The important part is "We will support all those who refuse to be conscripted."

Gentlemen of the jury, the scene in this court has been a quiet one. It has been the aim of the defendants to convey to your mind the impression that it would have been absolutely inconsistent that they should even have advocated such terrible things as they are charged with. Gentlemen of the jury, you have not been at the different mass meetings that I have been compelled to attend. But I think you have a pretty fair picture in your mind. You have at those mass meetings a very different Emma Goldman, for example, than the Emma Goldman who in this court says "Thank you" to witnesses. You have there the emotional Emma Goldman, something as you heard to-day, with all that fiery oratory that makes her so dangerous to the peace and security of the United States. Anybody who underestimates Emma Goldman's oratory, anybody who underestimates Emma Goldman's intellectual qualities is a fool. She is the best speaker that you perhaps ever heard. And that is why her influence is so pernicious.

And the Alexander Berkman you have seen here—how he controlled himself in court! But you got a taste once of his other self: once he lost control of himself and protested against something that was "a damned outrage," as he termed it, but which was really a perfectly proper piece of legal procedure, the offer of something in Miss Goldman's handwriting, and His Honor admitted it. That is the Berkman who speaks at the meetings. Those are the people who are plotting from day to day against the peace and security of the United States and who impose their personalities upon the weak minds of ignorant foreigners who come to this country, come from persecution in Russia, and instead of being taught that they should give credit to this country for freedom of worship, freedom of education, they are taught that they ought to bring about a rebellion against this country, the same as they were taught in Russia to bring about rebellions against the tyrannous rule of the Czar.

Now, gentlemen of the jury, there is another element in this case injected by the defense. It really has nothing to do with the case, but it really calls for some explanation. You have been told by numerous witnesses that the soldiers and the police and the detectives tried to break up the meetings. Now, gentlemen of the jury, that has nothing to do with the question of fact as to whether these people conspired to cause people not to register, to aid and abet those who did not register. But it does show the psychology of the minds of these defendants, and I think it will interest you to bear this point in mind. But before I want to call it to your attention that these people came on the platforms and used expressions and indulged in attacks that they know are calculated to bring about a breach of the peace. They indulged in language that of itself constitutes disorderly conduct because it tends toward a breach of the peace.

Gentlemen of the jury, can you blame these young men in uniform who have enlisted in their country's service, who are ready to lay down their lives in defense of the principles upon which this Government is founded and for which it stands, who have to sit there and listen to people of this kind insult the President of the United States, defy the laws of the United States, desecrate the national emblem and heap ridicule upon the national anthem? Is it any wonder that the bonds of restraint must break when the people of this sort will presume beyond the endurance of a normal, free American citizen?

There was injected into the evidence something of a personal nature that I am sorry crept in—of course it doesn't make any difference—because it puts my personality in the case, where it doesn't belong. Miss Fitzgerald told you that at the meeting at the Royal Lyceum, on June 11th, Miss Goldmann came out of the hall and told me they were holding up registration cards of men over the conscriptable age; and I told her I had nothing to do with it, that I wasn't the marshal nor a policeman. She did say to me, according to the conceded testimony, "Well, you act like a policeman." Then I replied, "Well, if I were I might lock you up," or something of that sort. Now, that has nothing to do with the case, but it is perfectly apparent that Miss Goldman was trying to get into an argument—because that is their stock in trade, to get the other fellow's goat. And I am sorry to confess that one day they did get my goat and I had to apologize to the Court, because I fell a victim to the snare they had been laying for twenty-five years. They want you to fall for their snare, and then they blame it on you.

Gentlemen of the jury, in conclusion I want to say that this is a representative government. Before a law becomes the final law of the land every citizen through his chosen representative in Congress has the undoubted right to write to his Congressman, to see his Congressman and to take a definite stand on any piece of proposed legislation. Further than that, after a law is passed, if it appears to be a pernicious law every citizen has the undoubted right to urge the repeal of that law. But will you please tell me where in all the literature that has been offered in evidence, in all the speeches that have been offered in evidence, is there one word about proposed repeal of the conscription law? If these meetings were held merely to bring about the repeal of the conscription law, then why don't they say so? Can't you see that these people's object was wilfully to violate a law that was passed? If you don't believe in capital punishment, as you have a right not to believe in it, you have a right to agitate in the State of New York, if you will, for a repeal of the death penalty. If you do believe in the abolition of capital punishment, does that entitle you to go out and tell John Jones to murder somebody? That's a poor way to have a law repealed. That's precisely what these people have done. They don't like the conscription law. They don't like any law. But they are banded together, not to secure the repeal of that law, not to petition Congress in an orderly fashion, but to set themselves and their cohorts above the law of the United States. You were asked, gentlemen of the jury, if you believed in democracy. And every one of you believes in democracy. So does every one in this country believe in democracy. On the field of Gettysburg the immortal Lincoln said, "This is a government of the people, by the people and for the people." And so it is. The shadow of the great conflict at Gettysburg has passed off, but to-day this country stands north and south alike united in the defense of our common liberties. It is a government of the people, by the people and for the people. But an orderly government, a government of decent men and organized society, founded upon order and not upon chaos and Anarchy. And I say to you, gentlemen of the jury, that the sort of democracy for which Washington and Jefferson and Madison and Jackson and Lincoln fought and bled, that great democracy, that great orderly republican government must not succumb to and shall not be destroyed by the attacks of people like these two defendants who seek to abolish that very democracy that our forefathers have laid down their lives in defense of. That is the point. Of course we believe in democracy; but we don't propose to have that glorious democracy destroyed by Anarchy and bloodshed and violence.

Now, gentlemen of the jury, this case is an important case. That's doubtless why you have been so patient. It's an important case from the point of view of the defense. Nobody wants to underestimate the importance. But, gentlemen of the jury, this case is very important for the United States of America. As I said before, the Government of the United States is the district in which you participate through your duly constituted representatives. And this case is of prime importance to that Government. Will you by your verdict say that people like these can go forth again, defy our laws, desecrate the Stars and Stripes, make fun of the national anthem and do that with impunity? Urge people wilfully to set themselves above the provisions of a definite law? Aid and abet people who will not register for conscription? Are you by your verdict going to say that to them?

Or rather, gentlemen of the jury, are you going to say this: It has been shown that you two people got together in a common unlawful plan; that the object of your plan was to bring about that young men of conscriptable age should wilfully refuse to register as provided by law, and that you aided and abetted them in their unlawful activities, and that in pursuance of that conspiracy you did many outward acts looking toward the accomplishment of your wicked designs? Are you not rather going to say by your verdict, in these times when men are willing to give their treasure in behalf of those principles for which we all stand, and are willing to lay down their lives in behalf of the nation we love:

Strike till the last armed foe expires!
Strike for your altars and your fires!
Strike for the green graves of your sires!
God and your native land!

The Court's Charge

GENTLEMEN OF THE JURY: It is with real sincerity that I express to you my appreciation of the patience that you have displayed throughout this trial, and of the very close and intelligent attention that you have given to the testimony as it was adduced, and to the summing-up of the defendants and of the counsel for the prosecution. It is extremely important to concentrate your minds upon the particular question here involved, arising out of the indictment of these two defendants. They are charged by the grand jury with an offense which I shall more technically define later, which in effect is this: that they have knowingly and wilfully counseled, abetted and aided persons of the so-called "draft age" to violate a statute of the United States, against the peace and dignity of the United States. * * *

This is not a trial of political principles. This cannot be turned into a political or State trial in the political sense. You are not to be misled by any effort to digress your minds from the real issue, which simply is whether these defendants are guilty or not guilty of the crime charged in the indictment. This is not a question of free speech. Free speech is guaranteed to us under the Constitution. No American worthy of the name believes in else than free speech. But free speech means not license, not counseling disobedience of law. Free speech means that frank, fair, full and orderly expression which every man or woman in the land, citizen or alien, may engage in, in lawful and orderly fashion. And that free speech is guaranteed to us, and no court could deny it to anyone.

Prior to the enactment of the so-called selective service law, aptly designated such by the President, on the 18th day of May, 1917, any person could discuss in the fullest manner possible the provisions of the pending legislation. And any person in discussing that legislation could use even the most vehement language and present any and all arguments that seemed to him or to her best. But when that discussion becomes embodied into law, then it becomes the duty of every person living under this Government to obey that law. Individual opinion might still be fully expressed. Proper agitation for repeal might still continue. But the law itself thenceforth must be obeyed. This is a republic founded upon principles of democracy. It can remain a republic only as the law is obeyed. The obedience to law is the fundamental basis of American life. Once that basis disappears or is destroyed, the whole fabric is destroyed and the foundation upon which a government of free men rests, disappears. * * *

I may only say one thing more, concerning which there

can be little difference of opinion. Whatever may have been the fate of persons of historical note, whether the acts that they committed were within or without the law, is quite immaterial in this case. This is a country of law and order. The law must be obeyed. We are not dealing with a discussion of abstract principles. We are not concerned with the views of the defendants, whether they are right or wrong, on matters foreign to this case. We are only concerned with the evidence in the case. If you believe them guilty beyond a reasonable doubt, it is a matter of no concern to you nor to the court what their views may be. If you believe them not guilty, then equally are we not concerned with their political views.

I repeat in conclusion and lay it upon you most earnestly that this is not a trial of free speech. This is an indictment for crime. And the duty which rests upon you is to determine on the evidence whether or not the defendants are guilty or innocent of the crime charged in the indictment. Much has been said by the defendants and by the counsel for the Government as to what the country may think of your verdict. Gentlemen, we are within the solemn confines of a court. All the country wants from you is a just verdict on the evidence, a verdict that I know you will render, because you have given such close attention. And confining yourselves to that, it is your duty by deliberate consideration to arrive at a conclusion on the evidence and not to permit yourselves, as I am sure you will not, to be diverted into any attack—to make it seem as if any person were here on trial for the expression of opinion. The sole question is, has the Government proved the guilt of the defendants beyond a reasonable doubt? If so, your verdict is guilty. If not, your verdict is not guilty.

The Verdict

The jury retired at 5:20 and at 6 o'clock returned a verdict of guilty.

EMMA GOLDMAN: We move to set aside the verdict as being against the weight of evidence.

THE COURT: The stenographer may note that the motion is made, with formalities to cover all grounds upon which a motion to set aside a verdict may be made.

EMMA GOLDMAN: I wish to ask that sentence be deferred for a few days and that the present bail be continued meantime, because we want to arrange our affairs, which we have not had time to do during the trial.

THE COURT: The motion to set the verdict aside is denied.

MR. CONTENT: The Government moves for sentence.

And the Government feels in a case of public importance like this case that the judgment and mandate of the Court should be speedily handed down.

THE CLERK: Alexander Berkman to the bar! Is there any reason why the sentence of the Court should not now be pronounced upon you?

ALEXANDER BERKMAN: Well, I think that it is only fair to suspend sentence to give us a chance to arrange our affairs. And the fundamental reason why sentence should not be pronounced is that we are innocent of the charge and we are convicted as Anarchists, out of prejudice and bitterness. That's all.

THE CLERK: Miss Goldman, have you anything to say why sentence should not be imposed?

EMMA GOLDMAN: I wish to say that the very fact that we are refused to have sentence deferred for several days to arrange our affairs proves that the Court is prejudiced because we are Anarchists; because we were frank and because we stood by our opinions, and because we are going to stand by our opinions.

THE COURT: Gentlemen of the jury, I wish you would remain, for I desire to say before I may forget it that I think the appreciation of the Court and the community is due to you for the fearless and prompt manner in which you have discharged your duty.

It has undoubtedly been a source of regret to the gentlemen of the jury, as it has been to the Court and possibly to those who have sat in the courtroom for these many days, that the extraordinary ability displayed by the defendants has not been utilized in support of law and order. The magnetic power of one of the defendants, if thus utilized, might have been of great service, in forms legitimately advocated, for the betterment of conditions as the world goes on. That power might have been of tremendous service, and more especially among the millions of humbler people who come to our country in an aspiration for liberty. I understand, I think, what has been spoken of as the psychology of the defendants, and I am quite sure that they understand what might be called the psychology of the Court. We do represent the existing order of things, in-so-far as that means that progress must be accomplished in this country by lawful means. We regard as enemies of the Government in the most serious sense of that term those who advocate the abolition of this Government, those who counsel disobedience to our laws and those who induce the less strong-minded to disobey our laws. These may be very old and to some very tiresome sentiments. But they are the sentiments that from our point of view have become a part of our lives, won at great expense by the Revolutionary Fathers, by the men who fought in the great civil conflict and by the men who now are willing to stand by their country when their country needs them.

We have no place in this country for those who express the view that the law may be disobeyed in accordance with the thoughts of an individual. I am expressing not my view alone, I am expressing the view of what we in America understand to be the views of a true democracy and a true republic. The Government has thus far enacted no special statute to deal with those who counsel disobedience and who advise insurrection; who seek to reach and control the humbler people, some of whom don't understand things, by methods such as were disclosed in this case. And I desire, so far as I am concerned, that my words shall be perfectly understood, not merely by those who are here but by anyone else who has in his mind that he is stronger than the law. It makes very little difference what becomes of a single administrator of the law, whether he be officer, marshal, district attorney or judge. They come and go. But in this country the law is an imperishable thing that lives forever. And it merely uses for the moment as its administrators some human beings who may at any time give way to others. And so, when I impose this sentence I am imposing it on the one hand with regret that these abilities were not better used. I impose it on the other hand with profound conviction that I am speaking for organized law, for the kind of liberty that we know and we understand, who have been privileged to live in this country that we believe is a true democracy. The maximum sentence under the statute is two years and $10,000 fine. I sentence the defendant Alexander Berkman to the United States penitentiary in Atlanta for two years and fine him the sum of $10,000.

I sentence the defendant Emma Goldman to the State penitentiary at Jefferson City, Mo., for two years and fine her the sum of $10,000.

I further direct the District Attorney under the provisions of the immigration act to forward to the Commissioner of Labor the record of this conviction, in order to determine in due course whether or not either or both of the defendants are subject to the provisions as to deportation provided in that act. That is a matter which is under the statute, an administrative matter for the Commissioner of Labor. And the District Attorney is directed to forward the record of this conviction to the Commissioner of Labor.

The Court is now adjourned without day.

EMMA GOLDMAN: Just one moment, please. We wish to ask—as we intend to appeal the case—whether we may have time to consult with counsel and to proceed with the preparation of the appeal.

THE COURT: Under our rule you have ninety days within which to sue out a writ of error. And in order that there may be no mistake or confusion on the subject, the stenographer will note that the defendants may have ninety days within which to sue out a writ of error.

EMMA GOLDMAN: We should however like to know more specifically whether we may, after we are taken away from here, consult regarding the appeal or whether we are to be spirited away in a speedy manner. We would like to know that, to be quite clear where we stand.

THE COURT: The fullest opportunity within the ninety days will be given to the defendants to consult counsel and prepare their assignments of error and their writ of error. If in the course of that period there is no such opportunity, the defendants can address a communication to the Court and the Court will see that such an opportunity is afforded them. As a matter of fact, such opportunity is your right at any time within ninety days.

EMMA GOLDMAN: May I just ask what the procedure is, regarding whether we can now—I mean within the next hour or two—consult with counsel about our appeal? We ought to know that.

THE COURT: The custody of the defendants is with the Marshal, and the Marshal will attend to the matter referred to. Court is now adjourned.

EMMA GOLDMAN: I wish to thank the Court for the marvelous fair trial we have received. History will record, Your Honor, that two people asked for an adjournment, or rather deferring of sentence, of two days to arrange their affairs, and yet the Court considered them so dangerous to the United States that it would not even give them two days—which are given to the most heinous criminal. Thank you very much.

Notwithstanding the Judge's statement that it was the defendants' right to have ninety days in which to prepare their appeal, Emma Goldman and Alexander Berkman were taken away from New York on the same evening and rushed, on midnight trains, to the penitentiaries at Jefferson City, Mo., and Atlanta, Ga.

Testimony for the Defense

During the examination of the numerous witnesses for the defense, excerpts from various essays and articles, written by Alexander Berkman and Emma Goldman, were read by them to the jury for the purpose of clarifying their attitude on Anarchism and related subjects. Among the matter read was the following:

PREPAREDNESS: THE ROAD TO UNIVERSAL SLAUGHTER

[Read by Emma Goldman, from her pamphlet on Preparedness]

With the cunning methods used by the scheming diplomats and military cliques of Germany to saddle the masses with Prussian militarism, the American military ring with its Roosevelts, its Garrisons, its Daniels, and lastly its Wilsons, are moving the very heavens to place the militaristic heel upon the necks of the American people, and, if successful, will hurl America into the storm of blood and tears now devastating the countries of Europe.

Forty years ago Germany proclaimed the slogan: "Germany above everything. Germany for the Germans, first, last and always. We want peace; therefore we must prepare for war. Only a well armed and thoroughly prepared nation can maintain peace, can command respect, can be sure of its national integrity." And Germany began to prepare, thereby forcing the other nations to do the same. The terrible European war is only the culminating fruition of the hydra-headed gospel—military preparedness.

Since the war began, miles of paper and oceans of ink have been used to prove the barbarity, the cruelty, the oppression of Prussian militarism. Conservatives and radicals alike are giving their support to the Allies for no other reason than to help crush that militarism, in the presence of which, they say, there can be no peace or progress in Europe. But though America grows fat on the manufacture of munitions and war loans to the Allies to help crush Prussianism, the same cry is now being raised in America which, if carried into national action, would build up an American militarism far more terrible than German or Prussian militarism could ever be, and that because nowhere in the world has capitalism become so brazen in its greed and nowhere is the State so ready to kneel at the feet of capital.

The very proclaimers of "America first" have long before this betrayed the fundamental principles of real Americanism, of the kind of Americanism that Jefferson had in mind when he said that the best government is that which governs least; the kind of Americanism that David Thoreau worked for when he proclaimed that the best government is the one that doesn't govern at all; or the other truly great Americans who aimed to make of this country a haven of refuge, who hoped that all the disinherited and oppressed people in coming to these shores would give character, quality and meaning to the country. That is not the America of the politician and munition speculators. Their America is powerfully portrayed in the idea of a young New York sculptor I know: a hard cruel hand with long, lean, merciless fingers crushing in over the heart of the immigrant, squeezing out its blood in order to coin dollars and give the foreigner blighted hopes and stulted aspirations instead.

No doubt Woodrow Wilson has reason to defend these institutions. But what an ideal to hold out to the young generation! How is a military drilled and trained people to defend freedom, peace and happiness? This is what Major General O'Ryan has to say of an efficiently trained generation:

"The soldier must be so trained that he becomes a mere automaton; he must be so trained that it will destroy his initiative; he must be so trained that he is turned into a machine. The soldier must be forced into the military noose; he must be jacked up; he must be ruled by his superiors with pistol in hand."

This was not said by a Prussian Junker; not by a German barbarian: not by Treitschke or Bernhardi, but by an American Major General. And he is right. You cannot conduct war with equals; you cannot have militarism with free born men; you must have slaves, automatons, machines, obedient disciplined creatures, who will move, act, shoot and kill at the command of their superiors. That is preparedness, and nothing else.

I am no more pro-German than pro-Ally. As an Anarchist I refute both, as the "two thieves who are too cowardly to fight." Hence they force the people to do their criminal deed, hence they sacrifice "the boys from every village, hamlet and town."

That which has driven the masses of Europe into the trenches and to the battlefields is not their inner longing for war; it must be traced to the cut-throat competition for military equipment, for more efficient armies, for larger warships, for more powerful cannon. You cannot build up a standing army and then throw it back into a box like tin soldiers. Armies equipped to the teeth with weapons, with highly developed instruments of murder and backed by the military interests, have their own dynamic functions. We have but to examine into the nature of militarism to realize the truism of this contention.

Militarism consumes the strongest and most productive elements of each nation. Militarism swallows the largest part of the national revenue. Almost nothing is spent on education, art, literature and science, compared with the amount devoted to militarism in times of peace, while in times of war everything else is set at naught; all life stagnates, all effort is curtailed; the very sweat and blood of the masses are used to feed this insatiable monster—militarism. Under such circumstances, it must become more arrogant, more aggressive, more bloated with its own importance. If for no other reason, it is out of surplus energy that militarism must act to remain alive; therefore it will seek an enemy or create one artificially. In this civilized purpose and method, militarism is sustained by the State, protected by the laws of the land, is fostered by the home and the school, and glorified by public opinion. In other words, the function of militarism is to kill. It cannot live except through murder.

But the most dominant factor of military preparedness and the one which inevitably leads to war, is the creation of group interests, which consciously and deliberately work for the increase of armament whose purposes are furthered by creating the war hysteria. This group interest embraces all those engaged in the manufacture and sale of munition and in military equipment for personal gain and profit. The family Krupp, for instance, which owns the largest cannon munition plant in the world; its sinister influence in Germany, and in fact in many other countries, extends to the press, the school, the church and to statesmen of highest rank. Shortly before the war, Carl Liebknecht, one of the few brave public men in Germany now, brought to the attention of the Reichstag that the family Krupp had in its employ officials of the highest military position, not only in Germany, but in France and in other countries. Everywhere its emissaries have been at work, systematically inciting national hatred and antagonisms; creating invasion hysteria.

It is not at all unlikely that the history of the present war will trace its origin to the same international murder trust. But is it always necessary for one generation to wade through oceans of blood and heap up mountains of human sacrifice that the next generation may learn a grain of truth from it all? Can we of to-day not profit by the cause which led to the European war, can we not learn that it was preparedness, thorough and efficient preparedness on the part of Germany and the other countries for military aggrandizement and material gain; above all can we not realize that preparedness in America must and will lead to the same result, the same barbarity, the same senseless sacrifice of life? Is America to follow suit, is it to be turned over to the American Krupps, the American military cliques? It almost seems so when one hears the jingo howls of the press, the blood and thunder tirades of the bully Roosevelt, the sentimental twaddle of our college-bred President.

The more reason for those who still have a spark of libertarianism and humanity left to cry out against this great crime, against the outrage now being prepared and imposed upon the American people. It is not enough to claim being neutral; a neutrality which sheds crocodile tears with one eye and keeps the other riveted upon the profits from war supplies and war loans, is not neutrality. It is a hypocritical cloak to cover the country's crimes. Nor is it enough to join the bourgeois pacifists who proclaim peace among the nations while helping to perpetuate the war among the classes, a war which, in reality, is at the bottom of all other wars.

It is this war of the classes that we must concentrate upon, and in that connection the war against false values, against evil institutions, against all social atrocities. Those who appreciate the urgent need of co-operating in great struggles must oppose military preparedness imposed by the State and capitalism for the destruction of the masses. They must organize the preparedness of the masses for the overthrow of both capitalism and the State. Industrial and economic preparedness is what the workers need. That alone leads to revolution at the bottom as against mass destruction from on top. That alone leads to true internationalism of labor against Kaiserdom, Kingdom, diplomacies, military cliques and bureaucracy. That alone will give the people the means to take their children out of the slums, out of the sweat shops and the cotton mills. That alone will enable them to inculcate in the coming generation a new ideal of brotherhood, to rear them in play and song and beauty; to bring up men and women, not automatons. That alone will enable woman to become the real mother of the race, who will give to the world creative men, and not soldiers who destroy. That alone leads to economic and social freedom, and does away with all wars, all crimes, and all injustice.

THE PSYCHOLOGY OF POLITICAL VIOLENCE

[Read by Emma Goldman, from her pamphlet bearing the same title]

Björnstjerne Björnson, in the second part of *Beyond Human Power*, emphasizes the fact that it is among the Anarchists that we must look for the modern martyrs who pay for their faith with their blood, and who welcome death with a smile, because they believe, as truly as Christ did, that their martyrdom will redeem humanity.

"There is a truism that the man in the street seems always to forget, when he is abusing the Anarchists, or whatever party happens to be his *bête noire* for the moment, as the cause of some outrage just perpetrated. This indisputable fact is that homicidal outrages have, from time immemorial, been the reply of goaded and desperate classes, and goaded and desperate individuals, to wrongs from their fellow-men, which they felt to be intolerable. Such acts are the violent recoil from violence, whether aggressive or repressive; they are the last desperate struggle of outraged and exasperated human nature for breathing space and life. And their cause lies not in any special conviction, but in the depths of that human nature itself. The whole course of history, political and social, is strewn with evidence of this fact. To go no further, take the three most notorious examples of political parties goaded into violence during the last fifty years: the Mazzinians in Italy, the Fenians in Ireland, and the Terrorists in Russia. Were these people Anarchists? No. Did they all three even hold the same political opinions? No. The Mazzinians were Republicans, the Fenians political separatists, the Russians Social Democrats or Constitutionalists. But all were driven by desperate circumstances into this terrible form of revolt. And when we turn from parties to individuals who have acted in like manner, we stand appalled by the number of human beings goaded and driven by sheer desperation into conduct obviously violently opposed to their social instincts.

Now that Anarchism has become a living force in society, such deeds have been sometimes committed by Anarchists, as well as by others. For no new faith, even the most essentially peaceable and humane the mind of man has yet accepted, but at its first coming has brought upon earth not peace, but a sword; not because of anything violent or anti-social in the doctrine itself; simply because of the ferment any new and creative idea excites in men's minds, whether they accept or reject it. And a conception of Anarchism, which, on one hand, threatens every vested interest, and, on the other, holds out a vision of a free and noble life to be won by a struggle against existing wrongs, is certain to rouse the fiercest opposition, and bring the whole repressive force of ancient evil into violent contact with the tumultuous outburst of a new hope.

Under miserable conditions of life, any vision of the possibility of better things makes the present misery more intolerable, and spurs those who suffer to the most energetic struggles to improve their lot, and if these struggles only immediately result in sharper misery, the outcome is sheer desperation. In our present society, for instance, an exploited wage worker, who catches a glimpse of what work and life might and ought to be, finds the toilsome routine and the squalor of his existence almost intolerable; and even when he has the resolution and courage to continue steadily working his best, and waiting until new ideas have so permeated society as to pave the way for better times, the mere fact that he has such ideas and tries to spread them, brings him into difficulties with his employers. How many thousands of Socialists, and above all Anarchists, have lost work and even the chance of work, solely on the ground of their opinions! It is only the specially gifted craftsman, who, if he be a zealous propagandist, can hope to retain permanent employment. And what happens to a man with his brain working actively with a ferment of new ideas, with a vision before his eyes of a new hope dawning for toiling and agonizing men, with the knowledge that his suffering and that of his fellows in misery is not caused by the cruelty of fate, but by the injustice of other human beings,—what happens to such a man when he sees those dear to him starving, when he himself is starved? Some natures in such a plight, and those by no means the least social or the least sensitive, will become violent, and will even feel that their violence is social and not anti-social, that in striking when and how they can, they are striking, not for themselves, but for human nature, outraged and despoiled in their persons and in those of their fellow sufferers. And are we, who ourselves are not in this horrible predicament, to stand by and coldly condemn these piteous victims of the Furies and Fates? Are we to decry as miscreants these human beings who act with heroic self-devotion, sacrificing their lives in protest, where less social and less energetic natures would lie down and grovel in abject submission to injustice and wrong? Are we to join the ignorant and brutal outcry which stigmatizes such men as monsters of wickedness, gratuitously running amuck in a harmonious and innocently peaceful society? No! We hate murder with a hatred that may seem absurdly exaggerated to apologists for Matabele massacres, to callous acquiescers in hangings and bombardments, but we decline in such cases of homicide, or attempted homicide, as those of which we are treating, to be guilty of the cruel injustice of flinging the whole responsibility of the deed upon the immediate perpetrator. The guilt of these homicides lies upon every man and woman who, intentionally or by cold indifference, helps to keep up social conditions that drive human beings to despair. The man who flings his whole life into the attempt at the cost of his own life, to protest against the wrongs of his fellow-men, is a saint compared to the active and passive upholders of cruelty and injustice, even if his protest destroy other lives besides his own. Let him who is without sin in society cast the first stone at such a one."

* * * * *

That every act of political violence should nowadays be attributed to Anarchists is not at all surprising. Yet it is a fact known to almost everyone familiar with the Anarchist movement that a great number of acts, for which Anarchists had to suffer, either originated with the capitalist press or were instigated, if not directly perpetrated, by the police.

For a number of years acts of violence had been committed in Spain, for which the Anarchists were held responsible, hounded like wild beasts, and thrown into prison. Later it was disclosed that the perpetrators of these acts were not Anarchists, but members of the police department. The scandal became so widespread that the conservative Spanish papers demanded the apprehension and punishment of the gang-leader, Juan Rull, who was subsequently condemned to death and executed. The sensational evidence, brought to light during the trial, forced Police Inspector Momento to exonerate completely the Anarchists from any connection with the acts committed during a long period. This resulted in the dismissal of a number of police officials, among them Inspector Tressols, who, in revenge, disclosed the fact that behind the gang of police bomb-throwers were others of far higher position, who provided them with funds and protected them.

* * * * *

"Repression, tyranny, and indiscriminate punishment of innocent men have been the watchwords of the government of the alien domination in India ever since we began the commercial boycott of English goods. The tiger qualities of the British are much in evidence now in India. They think that by the strength of the sword they will keep down India! It is this arrogance that has brought about the bomb, and the more they tyrannize over a helpless and unarmed people, the more terrorism will grow. We may deprecate terrorism as outlandish and foreign to our culture, but it is inevitable as long as this tyranny continues, for it is not the terrorists that are to be blamed, but the tyrants who are responsible for it. It is the only resource for a helpless and unarmed people when brought to the verge of despair. It is never criminal on their part. The crime lies with the tyrant."

* * * * *

Even conservative scientists are beginning to realize that heredity is not the sole factor moulding human character. Climate, food, occupation; nay, color, light, and sound must be considered in the study of human psychology.

If that be true, how much more correct is the contention that great social abuses will and must influence different minds and temperaments in a different way. And how utterly fallacious the stereotyped notion that the teachings of Anarchism, or certain exponents of these teachings, are responsible for the acts of political violence.

Anarchism, more than any other social theory, values human life above things. All Anarchists agree with Tolstoy in this fundamental truth: if the production of any commodity necessitates the sacrifice of human life, society should do without that commodity, but it cannot do without that life. That, however, nowise indicates that Anarchism teaches submission. How can it, when it knows that all suffering, all misery, all ills, result from the evil of submission?

Has not some American ancestor said, many years ago, that resistance to tyranny is obedience to God? And he was not an Anarchist even. I would say that resistance to tyranny is man's highest ideal. So long as tyranny exists, in whatever form, man's deepest aspiration must resist it as inevitably as man must breathe.

Compared with the wholesale violence of capital and government, political acts of violence are but a drop in the ocean. That so few resist is the strongest proof how terrible must be the conflict between their souls and unbearable social iniquities.

High strung, like a violin, they weep and moan for life, so relentless, so cruel, so terribly inhuman. In a desperate moment the string breaks. Untuned ears hear nothing but discord. But those who feel the agonized cry understand its harmony; they hear in it the fulfillment of the most compelling moment of human nature.

Such is the psychology of political violence.

ASPIRATIONS OF THE BLAST

[Read by Alexander Berkman, from THE BLAST, Vol. 1, No. 2]

THE BLAST is not a decent, respectable paper. Decency and Respectability—Mother Grundy's bastard twins—change, like the fashions, with age, country and climate, mostly without rhyme or reason.

If you are a sissified mollycoddle of the good old kind that would put draping around a piano leg and go to bed in a night cap, drop this paper right now. It will surely shock you: for the truth is stark naked.

It is said: "The truth shall make you free." So it shall. But the truth is not a nugget found by luck. He who diligently searches will find grains of it now and then.

THE BLAST preaches no dogma. Its mission is more revolutionary: to arouse independence of feeling, thought and action, without which there is no road to human freedom.

Freedom is primarily a state of mind. It can neither be chained in a dungeon nor heralded from the throne. There is no royal road to it, though the pathways are many. THE BLAST proposes to discuss them.

Any man or movement enlisted in the battle for the right of the worker to the Earth and the fulness thereof will find in THE BLAST a fighting friend, regardless of regimental insignia.

THE BLAST has no time to split hairs over policies.

If an institution has the elements of slavery within it, we shall grill it, no matter how respectably moss-grown it has become with age.

If THE BLAST can aid in sweeping away the cobwebs of tradition, and call to life the vision of a better, freer world, without oppression and legalized theft, without soldiers and bloodshed, without priests and superstitions, without politicians and graft, plutocrats and paupers, we shall not have worked in vain.

We know our limitations.

We are not profound philosophers. Hence we refuse to be slaves to consistency.

We are not learned scholars. Therefore faulty rhetoric will not freeze the blood in our veins.

We are free from the blight of professional journalism. We shall not worry ourselves to death about style.

We are but workers with a passion for Freedom and with the determination to express it in the face of all difficulty and danger.

If you are with us, *now* is the time to prove your interest and solidarity.

VIOLENCE AND ANARCHISM

[Read by Alexander Berkman, from his article published in THE BLAST, Vol. I, No. 17]

It is growing rather monotonous to hear the cry of "Anarchist conspiracy" raised whenever and wherever there happens an "unlawful" shot or bomb explosion

Let us consider the matter dispassionately. Is violence specifically Anarchistic? Is the taking of human life such a very unusual occurrence among "civilized" peoples? Is our whole social existence anything but an uninterrupted series of murder, assassination, mutilation? All our honored institutions are rooted in the very spirit of murder. Do we build warships for educational purposes? Is the army a Sunday school? Our police, jails and penitentiaries—what purpose do they serve but to suppress, kill and maim? Is the gallows the symbol of our brotherhood, the electric chair the proof of our humanitarianism?

"All these things are necessary evils," we are told by the self-satisfied. True, they are necessary; necessary to preserve society *as it is*. But has it ever occurred to the "good citizen" whether it is really necessary to preserve things as they are? Is it indeed worth while?

Organized society can have but on *raison d'être;* namely, the greatest good of its members. Let us examine, then, whether society, as at present constituted, can be justly said to fulfill its mission.

No life, individual or collective, is possible without the means of subsistence. The social members supplying these means are, consequently, the life-givers of the community. And who are they? The question answers itself automatically: the producers of the country's wealth are the conservators of its life. All members and classes of society should equally benefit by the fact of our combined effort as a society. But if, for any reason, distinctions are to be made, the producing class, the real backbone of the social body, should have the preference.

In other words, the workers are the ones who should enjoy the greatest benefits arising from social organization. That is the true mission of human society. Does the latter accomplish it? Does it come anywhere near accomplishment?

By no means. The producers are the very ones on whose shoulders rests the whole burden of our social evils. They are the disinherited, the submerged. The products of their toil are the property of some one else; the land and machinery, without which no production is possible, are not owned by them; as a result, they are forced to sell their labor for whatever pittance the employers condescend to give. Hence poverty, starvation, and widespread misery among the very class which, as the sole producer, has the best claim to enjoy the blessings of organized social life.

To support, defend and perpetuate these unjust and terrible conditions it is necessary to have police, prisons, laws and government. For the disinherited are not content to forever starve in the midst of plenty, and the exploited are beginning to cry out against their cruel bondage.

These cries, these signs of rebellious dissatisfaction must be stifled. That is the mission of law and government: to preserve things as they are; to secure to the rich their stolen wealth; to strangle the voice of popular discontent.

Such is the social life of "civilized" countries. A life of misery and degradation, of economic exploitation, governmental suppression, legal brutality and judicial murder. Sham, injustice and tyranny are the synonyms of organized society. Shall we preserve it as it is? Is it necessary and desirable? Is it even possible?

"But you can't regenerate society by violence, by a bomb," the well-meaning people argue.

Indeed, full well we know we cannot. Be fair; give ear. Do not confound the philosophy of a better, freer and happier life with an *act resulting from the very evils which that philosophy seeks to abolish.*

Anarchism is the science of social order, as opposed to existing disorder; of brotherhood, as against present Ishmaelitism; of individual liberty and well-being, as opposed to legal oppression, robbery and universal misery.

This condition of social regeneration cannot be achieved by the will or act of any man or party. The enlightenment of the workers regarding the evils of wage slavery, the awakening of the public conscience to a clearer understanding of liberty and justice—these are the forces which will abolish all forms of bondage, political, economical and social, replacing present institutions by free co-operation and the solidarity of communal effort.

"But the bomb?" cry the judges in and out of court. The bomb is the echo of your cannon, trained upon our starving brothers; it is the cry of the murdered striker; 'tis the voice of hungry women and children; the shriek of the maimed and torn in your industrial slaughter houses; it is the dull thud of the policeman's club upon a defenseless head; 'tis the shadow of the crisis, the rumbling of suppressed earthquake—it is Desperation's lightning out of an atmosphere of degradation and misery that king, president and plutocrat have heaped upon humanity. *The bomb is the ghost of your past crimes.*

You may foam and legislate, arrest, imprison and deport. You may still further tighten the thumb-screws of persecution, erect more gallows, and build electric chairs. Pitiful fools! Thus was Christ crucified as a disturber of "Caesar's peace." Did Golgotha suppress his teaching? Have the unspeakable tortures of the Inquisition eradicated free thought? Did Louis XVI save his crown—or his head—by *lettre de cachet?* Has the cause of the Abolitionists been defeated by the judicial murder of John Brown?

"Our graves will speak louder than the voices you strangle!" In spite of all the strenuous governmental, capitalistic and journalistic efforts to misrepresent and suppress Anarchists and Anarchism—because of those efforts—the people will yet learn the truth.

A New Declaration of Independence

[Read by Emma Goldman, from her essay in MOTHER EARTH, Vol. IV., 1909-10]

When, in the course of human development, existing institutions prove inadequate to the needs of man, when they serve merely to enslave, rob, and oppress mankind, the people have the eternal right to rebel against, and overthrow, these institutions.

The mere fact that these forces—inimical to life, liberty, and the pursuit of happiness—are legalized by statute laws, sanctified by divine rights, and enforced by political power, in no way justifies their continued existence.

We hold these truths to be self-evident: that all human beings, irrespective of race, color, or sex, are born with the equal right to share at the table of life; that to secure this right there must be established among men economic, social, and political freedom; we hold further that government exists but to maintain special privilege and property rights; that it coerces man into submission and therefore robs him of dignity, self-respect, and life.

The history of the American kings of capital and authority is the history of repeated crimes, injustices, oppression, outrage, and abuse, all aiming at the suppression of individual liberties and the exploitation of the people. A vast country, rich enough to supply all her children with all possible comforts, and insure well-being to all, is in the hands of a few, while the nameless millions are at the mercy of ruthless wealth gatherers, unscrupulous lawmakers, and corrupt politicians. . Sturdy sons of America are forced to tramp the country in a fruitless search for bread, and many of her daughters are driven into the street, while thousands of tender children are daily sacrificed on the altar of Mammon. The reign of these kings is holding mankind in slavery, perpetuating poverty and disease, maintaining crime and corruption; it is fettering the spirit of liberty, throttling the voice of justice, and degrading and oppressing humanity. It is engaged in continual war and slaughter, devastating the country and destroying the best and finest qualities of man; it nurtures superstition and ignorance, sows prejudice and strife, and turns the human family into a camp of Ishmaelites.

We, therefore, the liberty-loving men and women, realizing the great injustice and brutality of this state of affairs, earnestly and boldly do hereby declare, That each and every individual is and ought to be free to own himself and to enjoy the full fruit of his labor; that man is absolved from all allegiance to the kings of authority and capital; that he has, by the very fact of his being, free access to the land and all means of production, and entire liberty of disposing of the fruits of his efforts; that each and every individual has the unquestionable and unabridgeable right of free and voluntary association with other equally sovereign individuals for economic, political, social, and all other purposes, and that to achieve this end man must emancipate himself from the sacredness of property, the respect for man-made law, the fear of the Church, the cowardice of public opinion, the stupid arrogance of national, racial, religious, and sex superiority, and from the narrow puritanical conception of human life. And for the support of this Declaration, and with a firm reliance on the harmonious blending of man's social and individual tendencies, the lovers of liberty joyfully consecrate their uncompromising devotion. their energy and intelligence, their solidarity and their lives.

Prison Memoirs Of An Anarchist

By Alexander Berkman

What the Reviews say of this book.

Berkman's book is noteworthy as a human document, an analysis of human emotions and a study of the subtle influence of environment material and psychic.—*Springfield (Mass.) Republican.*

For a quarter of a century past our standard of the misery of a prison life has been more or less definitely set by a record of a convict existence in Siberia. It may be that for those of us who read the new "Prison Memoirs of an Anarchist" a new high-water mark will be reached in our understanding of prison wretchedness. * * * In the book of his experience Berkman has given us a record of horrors that comes near being unsurpassed. We have here a picture of a hideous existence, hideous in its physical conditions, hideous in its moral degradation, hideous most of all in its madness. It is not in Siberia; it is in Pittsburgh. —*The N. Y. Times.*

Berkman was sent to the penitentiary and served his time. In this book he tells his story. And he tells it in a way that reminds you of Dostoyevsky and the other great Russian realists. Berkman is a staccato realist. He is an odd rationalist and emotionalist. But he gets himself over into your comprehension and does it completely. The writer is an artist—consciously or unconsciously. His big picture has an impressive background. And in the foreground is life, lighted by thought and moving in passion. Berkman is lyrical in his ecstasy. And yet in his ecstasy he sees clearly. His exposition of himself and his cause is a rare piece of psychology. Reading him, taking his point of view, you cannot call him a murderer. He knows how to tell his story. He tells it so you see it as a sort of working of something like Greek Fate. And it is that large conception of the drama of his deed that makes his book a big one. His narrative of his long years in prison is fascinating. What he suffered he makes plain. But he is never sorry for himself, always for his fellow-convicts, for mankind that has "sought out many inventions" that have brought prisons into existence. * * * Those who like the work of Tolstoy, of Turgenieff, of Gogol, of Dostoyevsky, of Gorky, of Andreyev, of Tchekov, will find in Berkman the brother of the men and women whose lives those authors tell.—*The St. Louis Mirror.*

Nothing could exceed the uncanny spell exercised by this story. A psychic and, whether conscious or not, a highly literary effect has been produced by the use throughout of the present tense. * * * Berkman has succeeded in making you live in his prison experiences with him, and his book is probably as complete a self-revelation as is humanly possible.—*N. Y. Evening Post.*

A story of prison life by an author who spent fourteen years behind the bars gathering his material ought to have value as a human document. When the writer, furthermore, wields his pen in the manner of the Slavic realists and is compared by critics with such men as Dostoyevsky and Andreyev, his work must possess a tremendous fascination as well as a social value.—*N. Y. Tribune.*

Price $1.50—Postage 15c

MOTHER EARTH PUBLISHING ASSOCIATION

226 Lafayette Street New York

Printed in Dunstable, United Kingdom

91220039R00060